CAREERS IN THE NEW ECONOMY™

CAREERS IN FITNESS AND PERSONAL TRAINING

RANDY
LITTLEJOHN

THE ROSEN PUBLISHING GROUP, INC,
NEW YORK

Dedicated to Jim Rohn who said, "Take care of your body. It's the only place you have to live."

Published in 2005 by The Rosen Publishing Group, Inc.
29 East 21st Street, New York, NY 10010

Library of Congress Cataloging-in-Publication Data

Littlejohn, Randy.
Careers in fitness and personal training/Randy Littlejohn.—1st ed.
    p. cm.—(Careers in the new economy)
Includes bibliographical references and index.
ISBN 1-4042-0248-X (library binding)
1. Physical education and training—Vocational guidance—United States. 2. Personal trainers—Vocational guidance—United States. I. Title. II. Series.
GV481.4.L55 2005
613.7'1'023—dc22

                                                        2004015472

Manufactured in the United States of America

Photo Credits: Cover, pp. 1, 3, 4–5, 17, 25, 35, 47, 57, 71, 78, 87, 93, 102, 114, 122, 137, 140, 142 © Comstock, Inc.

Designer: Nelson Sá; **Editor:** Annie Sommers;
Photo Researcher: Nelson Sá

CONTENTS

INTRODUCTION

If you love physical exercise, it may seem like working out and getting paid for it is a dream come true. Career fitness professionals can enjoy their jobs and gain financial independence at the same time. This book is a road map to career opportunities for fitness professionals.

One potential barrier is an unclear definition of what actually constitutes a fitness professional. To become a fitness professional, you'll have to decide precisely what that term means to you. If you desire to be a professional athlete, this is not the book for you. However, if helping people have fun achieving physical fitness appeals to you, this is the perfect book for you—and opportunity is everywhere.

Your second challenge is to define a career path. Compared with the steps outlined for becoming a certified public accountant, doctor, or lawyer, for example, the path to becoming a fitness professional is not as clear cut. Nevertheless, a career as a fitness professional is within your reach. All you need is some information, a desire to succeed, a passion for fitness, and the willingness to face a few challenges.

First, we'll look at some basic definitions. In general, fitness professionals plan, organize, and direct fitness activities. For example, these fitness activities may be resistance training for muscle fitness or muscle building (such as weight training) or aerobic conditioning exercises that specifically target the heart, lungs, and circulatory system. Fitness professionals may also develop specialized fitness

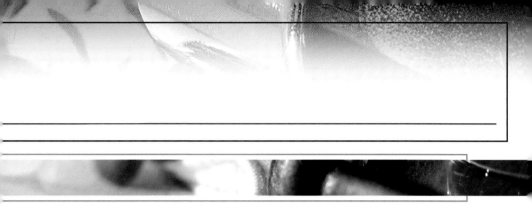

activities for the elderly, for the physically handicapped, or for those recovering from injuries.

People planning a fitness career should be outgoing, good at motivating people, and sensitive to the physical and mental strengths and limitations of others. Excellent health and physical fitness are required because of the physical nature of the job. As in many fields, leadership skills are needed for advancing to supervisory or management positions. Even self-employed fitness professionals would be well served by basic business and supervisory skills.

Professional fitness workers find jobs in community centers, health clubs, fitness centers, retirement centers, rehabilitation centers, on board cruise ships, and in many other places where they can help people overcome physical limitations. They work with people of all ages. As we move further into the twenty-first century, large corporate employers have found that healthy workers are happier and more productive. They also take far fewer sick days. Hence, fitness professionals can also be found in corporate workplaces, where they organize and direct athletic programs for employees.

Fitness professionals typically specialize in a few areas covered by certification programs and/or a college or university degree program. By investigating available certification and other educational programs, you can decide which specialty areas interest you. Maybe you're most interested in people who like to dance. Maybe you only want to work with young or elderly people. Maybe you like physical fitness, but you're more interested in the business end of things. Maybe you love fitness but also love biology and anatomy. In this case, your choices may lead you to work with people who are recovering from injuries. There are many ways in which the fitness industry can accommodate whatever area of the field you are interested in.

For example, an aerobics instructor conducts group exercise sessions involving aerobic exercise, stretching, and muscle conditioning. A group fitness instructor teaches and leads groups of people in aerobic exercise, stretching, and muscle conditioning. However, he or she is also specially trained to help clients assess their levels of physical fitness and to help them set and reach specific fitness goals. For example, if you want to lose weight or gain muscle mass, a group fitness instructor is trained to help you get the results you want. Group fitness instructors help people refine their training techniques. They keep records of their clients' exercise sessions so that their progress toward physical fitness can be analyzed.

Personal trainers are similarly trained, but they work with clients on a one-on-one basis in either a gym or at the client's home. While personal trainers, group fitness instructors, and aerobic instructors focus on exercise, wellness coaches are trained to go beyond simple exercises.

Wellness coaches help clients overcome mental, physical, dietary, or environmental barriers that prevent them from reaching their wellness goals. In Canada, a fitness consultant is a professional with expertise in many areas that are covered by both personal trainers and wellness coaches in the United States.

Personal trainers, wellness coaches, and fitness consultants look at a person's lifestyle, level of fitness, and wellness goals (physical fitness is only one part of wellness) and then work to form a plan that will suit each specific individual. For example, if you have a problem giving up fattening foods, are not disciplined enough to work out regularly, you live in a place where it's hard to find a gym, or you have a chronic problem like asthma or depression, these specialists will evaluate your lifestyle, your specific needs, where you live, and your personality (among other things), in order to create a specialized plan just for you.

Clinical exercise specialists work with people suffering from specific physical ailments. They design appropriate exercise programs for patients in accordance with their physicians' recommendations.

Fitness directors are managers at health clubs or fitness centers. Their work involves creating and maintaining fitness programs that meet the needs of the club's members. Some fitness professionals own small independent fitness centers. In this case, fitness professionals may find themselves doing more public relations, advertising, paperwork, and bookkeeping than actually training clients.

EMPLOYMENT AND JOB OUTLOOK

According to the current U.S. Department of Labor Bureau of Labor Statistics, most fitness trainers and aerobics instructors are employed at physical fitness facilities, health clubs, and community fitness centers. Some other employers of fitness workers include hotels and resorts, summer camps, cruise ships, fitness centers within apartment complexes, and, increasingly, internal corporate fitness centers. Other options are health care facilities and fitness research programs. Many fitness professionals are self-employed.

According to the *Occupational Outlook Handbook*, a publication of the U.S. Department of Labor, after a few years, skilled fitness professionals can earn up to $54,000 a year and more. However, earnings can vary. For instance, in some regions of the United States, pay is more than in other regions. This is generally because some regions of the country have a higher cost of living, whereas other areas are less expensive to live in. People with degrees generally make more than people without degrees. People who have extensive experience in the field earn more than those with little or no actual experience outside of a certification or college program.

The *Occupational Outlook Handbook* is a nationally recognized source of career information that is revised every two years. Look for a copy in the reference section of your public library. More information about the *Occupational Outlook Handbook*, including how to access it on the Internet and how to order a print version, can be found in the back of this book.

Fitness professionals who work for an employer can expect to receive health and vacation benefits. Fitness professionals who are self-employed (freelancers) are responsible for their own health plans and vacation pay. This is true of freelancers in any field.

Some specialty areas in the fitness field pay more, while others pay less. For instance, an aerobic instructor who does not have a college degree and does not have multiple fitness certifications may earn just enough money to live a modest lifestyle. Someone with a college degree in physical therapy who is also certified to be a clinical exercise specialist will likely make a very good living. A personal trainer whose clients are working actors, actresses, and producers in Hollywood can earn a great deal more than $54,000 a year. Successful fitness models who have their own lines of fitness programs on tape, CD, or DVD, or who have a line of fitness clothes or advertise on television, can make even more. If you are ambitious, there are practically no limits to how financially successful you can become. This is because what you will be selling is the very simple fact that, as Ralph Waldo Emerson (1803–1882) said, "The first wealth is health."

According to the *National Industry-Occupation Employment Matrix*, a publication of the U.S. Bureau of Labor Statistics, employment of fitness workers is expected to increase faster than average due to rising interest in personal training, aerobics instruction, and other fitness activities. A 40 percent increase in the number of employment opportunities for fitness and nutrition professionals is expected by 2010. (National employment projections are evaluated every other year.)

Projected job growth stems, in part, from rising demand for fitness activities for older adults in senior centers, retirement communities, and other settings. There are two reasons for this. People are living longer. Plus, a large group of people born in the years following World War II—the so-called baby boomers—is beginning to reach retirement age. In order to prevent many illnesses such as heart disease and arthritis, the general population has increasingly sought the benefits of exercise and its effects on overall health and well-being.

In addition, more workers will be needed to develop and lead activity programs in halfway houses for people recovering from mental illness, physical abuse or drug abuse, as well as in children's homes and day care programs for people with special needs. Furthermore, fitness jobs will continue to increase as more large corporations recognize the benefits of providing fitness programs and other services (such as wellness programs) for their employees. Job growth also will occur in athletic clubs.

WORKING CONDITIONS

Regardless of the setting, most fitness workers spend their time indoors in the homes of their clients or in brightly lit, air-conditioned gyms and fitness centers. Fitness directors and supervisors typically spend most of their time in an office. Here, they plan specialized fitness programs such as martial arts or kickboxing and special fitness events such as weight-lifting competitions, marathons, and community events. They generally engage in less physical activity than do lower-level fitness workers. Nevertheless, fitness workers at all levels risk suffering injuries during physical fitness activities. No matter how careful people in fitness programs are, there will be bruises, and sometimes muscles will be strained, ankles will be twisted, and fingers will get jammed.

Most fitness employees work about forty hours a week. People entering this field should expect to work some night and weekend shifts, as well as some irregular hours directing aerobic and/or weight-training classes. Most prime shifts go to those workers with the most experience.

A typical forty to fifty-hour week could break down as follows:

- 15 to 20 hours of hands-on personal training
- 5 to 10 hours of group fitness instructing (a steady and sure source of income)
- 15 to 20 hours of administrative work, such as scheduling, designing programs, billing clients, and advertising

TRAINING, QUALIFICATIONS, AND ADVANCEMENT

Generally, in order to work, fitness workers must obtain certification in the fitness field. There are many organizations and schools that offer fitness classes and certification testing for the many specific job areas in the fitness field, such as a group fitness instructor or clinical exercise specialist. Some of the oldest and best known include:

- Aerobics and Fitness Association of America (AFAA)
- American College of Sports Medicine (ACSM)

- American Council on Exercise (ACE)
- American Fitness Professionals and Associates (AFPA)
- International Fitness Professionals Association (IFPA)
- National Academy of Sports Medicine (NASM)
- National Dance-Exercise Instructors Training Association (NDEITA)
- National Strength and Conditioning Association (NSCA)
- Ontario Association of Sport and Exercise Sciences (OASES)
- The Canadian Association of Fitness Professionals (Can-Fit-Pro)
- The Canadian Society for Exercise Physiology (CSEP)

Each organization has a slightly different core philosophy. Some are targeted toward careers in a medical context, such as a clinical exercise specialist. Some, such as the American College of Sports Medicine, emphasize an in-depth scholarly approach. Meanwhile, others stick to the basics, while also addressing the practical skills necessary to start and run a new business. However, most cover the same basic studies. There is a more complete list of certifying organizations and schools in the back of this book.

In general, if you want to earn a fitness career certification, all you need to do is contact a certification organization and enroll. The back of this book includes a list of certifying organizations. Be aware that costs vary. Many students study at home and then travel to a nearby town for testing. Other careers in the fitness field require attendance at a college or university.

Students can expect to study basic theories of fitness, anatomy, physiology, biomechanics, nutrition, and weight management, as well as the practical applications of fitness instruction, including workout program design, leadership, and communication skills. Advanced courses may pertain to the fields of health, nutrition, injury prevention, and aerobic conditioning.

Fitness certifications are usually valid for one or two years, after which workers must become recertified. Recertification is accomplished by attending continuing education classes. Most fitness workers are required to maintain a cardiopulmonary resuscitation (CPR) certification. Some employers also require workers to be certified in first aid. When considering a certification association, here are some questions to consider:

- Is the program highly regarded in the field? You may want to take a trip to a few fitness centers in your area and ask managers or certified fitness instructors whom they would recommend and why.
- Inquire about renewal and recertification procedures. There is a list of certifying organizations listed in the back of this book.
- Is the association easy to contact? If you reach an association by phone, are you able to speak with someone right away? If you have to leave a message on voice mail, do you get a call back in a timely fashion? If you contact a certification association by e-mail, does someone promptly answer your questions? Are the people you contact polite and professional?
- Does the association have a toll-free number? Usually, if it is a large professional organization, it will have one.
- How long has the association been in business?
- Does the association have a physical location or is it available only on the Internet? If it is a large, professional organization, it will have a physical location listed.
- Is the program convenient? In other words, is it easy to get the study books and tests? Do you have to travel to the other side of the state/province to be tested, or

does the organization provide many convenient locations for testing?

- Does the association offer professional liability insurance?
- How many graduates does the association have on record? A large, established association will be happy to tell you. Do some comparisons. Which association seems to certify the most fitness professionals?
- Does the association provide support during and after your studies? For instance, does it have people whom you can call with questions? After you start working, does the association offer continuing education? Does it offer a network of other graduates whom you can contact?
- Where are their graduates working?

In the United States, five certifying agencies have joined together to create a standardized accreditation process. This allows certifying agencies to ensure the credibility of nationally recognized certification tests and to increase the credibility of the industry. The five certifying agencies are:

- The American Council on Exercise (ACE)
- Aerobics and Fitness Association of America (AFAA)
- American College of Sports Medicine (ACSM)
- National Academy of Sports Medicine (NASM)
- National Strength and Conditioning Association (NSCA)

These agencies are developing minimum competency requirements for certification exams as well as an accreditation process for certifying agencies. They are also looking at acquiring accreditation from a third party, such as the National Commission for Certifying Agencies (NCCA). The NCCA is the certifying arm of the National Organization for

Competency Assurance (NOCA). Currently, a third party has accredited a few certifying exams in the industry. One agency that has been accredited by the NOCA is the ACE.

The NOCA is the only national accreditation body for private certification organizations in all disciplines. Its goal is to measure the ability of certifying organizations in any industry in order to accurately discriminate between qualified and unqualified professionals. NOCA standards are tough as well as being time-consuming to meet. The application itself is several hundred pages long, and application time is about a year. After gaining approval, an organization must then work to maintain such a high standard.

While many jobs are available to those with fitness certifications, some employers in the United States are beginning to require that fitness workers have a bachelor's degree in fields related to health or fitness—for example, exercise science or physical education. Some employers allow workers to substitute a college degree for certification, while others require both a degree and certification. A bachelor's degree (and, in some cases, a master's degree in exercise science, physical education, or a related area), along with experience, is usually required for advancement toward management positions in a health club or fitness center. While some employers will substitute a college education for a fitness certification, it is not likely that an employer will be willing to hire someone with a fitness certificate when an applicant with a college or university degree is available. It is a good idea to keep this in mind: the more you know, the more you're worth. These are some other requirements that are often needed for jobs in today's fitness field:

- Strong written, verbal, presentation, and interpersonal communication skills

- A willingness to assist clients with proper and safe use of fitness equipment

Fitness Jobs and Their Associated Educational Requirements

Aerobics Instructor Certification: A current CPR certification and a college degree is suggested.

Aquatics Instructor Certification: A current CPR certification and a college degree is suggested.

Athletic Trainer: A bachelor's degree.

Biomechanist: A master's degree.

Cardiopulmonary Rehabilitation Specialist: The minimum is an undergraduate degree; an advanced degree plus a recognized certification is suggested.

Exercise Specialist: Experience in the fitness field designing and implementing exercise programs and/or an approved fitness-worker certification. A bachelor's degree in exercise science or a related field, and a current CPR certification.

Fitness-Club Owner: Experience working in a fitness club plus college-level education in business studies.

Fitness Director: A college degree in a health- or fitness-related field. At least two years of experience as a fitness manager, a current health-and/or fitness-instructor certification, and current CPR certification.

Group Fitness Instructor Certification: A current CPR certification and a college degree is suggested.

Personal Trainer Certification: A current CPR certification and a college degree is suggested.

Physical/Occupational Therapist: An undergraduate degree, plus two or three years of specific studies related to the activities of a physical/occupational therapist is suggested. This qualifies an individual to sit for the National Board for Certification in Occupational Therapy (NBCOT) certification exam.

Wellness Coach: Two years of experience as a health or fitness professional working with patients. At least an associate's degree, but preferably a bachelor's degree, in fields such as exercise or nutrition. A current CPR certification is also suggested.

- The ability to manage multiple tasks, such as tracking membership data and other business details
- Computer proficiency

Now that you have learned a little more about what fitness professionals do and how to become a fitness worker, we'll take a look at specific jobs in the fitness industry, such as aerobics instructor, group fitness instructor, personal trainer, wellness coach, clinical exercise specialist, fitness director, and owner of a small independent fitness center. Chapter 8 explores other careers that are possible with an advanced university degree.

CHAPTER 1

AEROBICS INSTRUCTOR

If getting paid to work out sounds like a good deal to you, you may be the right person to become an aerobics instructor. However, there may be more to the job than you think, and some training will be necessary.

Aerobics instructors prepare and conduct group exercise sessions that involve aerobic exercise, stretching, and muscle conditioning. They encourage and motivate participants while supervising technique. At the same time, a good instructor needs to ensure that clients receive the maximum benefit while avoiding injury. You will need to know how to adapt your exercise programs to the needs of a wide variety of people with varying skills and fitness levels.

As an aerobics instructor, you'll create your own choreography (a series of dancelike moves). These moves must be appropriate for both beginning and advanced students. Choreography that is too easy will bore some advanced clients, while choreography that is too complex will confuse beginning clients. It will be a good idea to create choreography that is modifiable so that both the newer students and the highly experienced ones have options.

What Is "Aerobic" Fitness?

The word "aerobic" means "with oxygen" or "in the presence of oxygen." Aerobic training is exercise that develops aerobic or cardiovascular conditioning. It refers to activities in which oxygen from the blood is required to fuel the energy-producing mechanisms of muscle fibers. Some examples are running, cycling, rowing, and cross-country skiing.

Aerobic activity taxes the heart, lungs, and vascular system (blood-carrying pathways) in order to process and deliver clean, oxygen-rich blood more quickly (and in greater volume) to every part of the body. The heart and lungs respond to aerobic exercise by becoming stronger and more efficient. This is a good thing because any increased demand on skeletal muscles (the kind that your arms and legs move) creates an increased need for oxygen-rich blood. The body also responds to aerobic conditioning by growing more pathways for blood to help support a greater demand from the muscles. The result is that an aerobically fit individual can work longer and more vigorously, and achieve a quicker recovery at the end of an aerobic workout session.

Another benefit is that aerobically fit people are less likely to be overweight or have problems later in life with heart disease and clogged arteries. These kinds of medical conditions do not only happen to the elderly. Heart disease and clogged arteries can appear in children who are not physically active. Researchers have also found that regular participation in aerobic exercise is associated with greater mental well-being. This includes fewer instances of depression and more efficient mental activity.

The movements that you teach not only need to be appropriate for all clients but also, and perhaps most important, they need to be safe. To be able to choreograph safe movements, you will need to study anatomy and kinesiology so that you understand how to work each body part without causing injuries. You also need to know some nutritional facts that play a part in physical fitness. An understanding of good nutrition helps an instructor be prepared to answer general questions such as, "How much protein should I eat?" or "What is the difference between simple and complex carbohydrates?" and

"Should I take nutritional supplements?" Most of all, an instructor needs to know when to refer clients to a specialist, such as a registered dietitian.

If you have the following qualities, you probably have the right stuff to be an aerobics instructor:

- You really love aerobics
- You have excellent health and physical fitness
- You are outgoing and enjoy sharing what you know with others
- You exhibit leadership skills and sensitivity
- You can motivate people

WORK ENVIRONMENT

Most aerobic instructors work indoors at fitness centers and health clubs. If you're just getting started, you can expect to work irregular hours and on some nights and weekends. The best hours are given to people with the most experience. If you are qualified to be an aerobics instructor, you will be a physically fit person with a good deal of knowledge about how to exercise safely. Nevertheless, the possibility of an exercise-related injury is an occupational hazard.

Keep in mind that you probably won't make a good living just by teaching aerobics. It would be physically stressful to do six classes every day, five days a week—and that is how many classes you would probably need to teach to makes ends meet. Specific income information is listed at the end of this chapter. In addition, health and fitness centers employ the majority of aerobic instructors on a part-time basis in order to keep costs down. Nevertheless, it's a great part-time job if you like getting paid to work out. As you add experience and education to your résumé, you will have the opportunity to move up into higher-paying jobs.

You are more likely to find full-time employment at a fitness center or a health club if you have multiple skills.

In between classes, you might work as part of the fitness floor staff. Fitness floor staff monitor equipment, supplies, and people in a fitness center. Depending on your other skills, you could also find yourself involved with sales and public relations.

Do I Need to Be Certified?

Ten years ago, anyone who looked good in a fitness outfit and wasn't afraid to get up in front of people could become an aerobics instructor. In the years since, the industry has grown and become educated. A great deal more is expected of today's instructors than looking fit and knowing a lot of choreography. Currently, there is no license required to be an aerobics instructor in the United States. However, to help guarantee your employability, it's a good idea to become certified. Most health and fitness clubs require that their instructors be certified. In Canada, there is also no legislation requiring certification to work as an aerobics instructor, but as in the United States, most employers require certification. There are, however, voluntary, industry-recommended provincial safety standards that employers are encouraged to abide by. These criteria may soon become national standards.

Modern aerobic dance classes have requirements that make them more than simple dance lessons. Depending on whether you are teaching high-low, step, kickboxing, or other group fitness styles, you will be expected to know exactly what you're doing. For instance, you'll need to be certain that your choreography equally works all major muscle groups. You'll be challenged to design workouts that are appropriate to the fitness levels of a wide variety of students. The music you choose must be the appropriate tempo, or beats per minute (BPM). If it is too fast, you could seriously harm your less-fit clients; if it is too slow, you won't be helping your clients increase their fitness level. How will you determine each client's fitness level? How will you know how to design a fitness program for clients at various levels ?

Training will give you the essentials for whichever style of aerobics you want to teach (and most instructors know several different styles). The Aerobic and Fitness Association of America (AFAA) has workshops for the most common group fitness classes, including step, kickboxing, and aquatics for seniors. These workshops are offered internationally, so you will most likely find one you can attend without having to travel too far. Ultimately, the more education you have, the more credibility you will earn and the more valuable you'll be as an employee.

Before starting an educational program in a fitness field, you may want to become certified for first aid and CPR. Often, employers of fitness workers require a fitness certification and certification for CPR and first aid. The American Heart Association and the Red Cross all provide programs. You will find contact information for these organizations in the back of this book.

CERTIFICATION

The Aerobics and Fitness Association of America is a major certifying body for aerobics instructors in the United States. A good place for Canadians to start would be the Canadian Association of Fitness Professionals (Can-Fit-Pro). Many other organizations provide certifications as well. See the back of this book for contact information.

The AFAA's basic certification for aerobics instructors is an excellent starting point for people just entering the field. There is no requirement for a college degree in a fitness-related field for the AFAA's basic aerobics instruction certification program. Exams include both written and practical components. The written exam consists of 100 multiple-choice and matching questions. The practical exam for the Primary Aerobic Certification includes a demonstration of how well you lead a group exercise class. Students are graded for appropriate warm-up, aerobic exercise, and muscle strengthening for the major muscle groups. The AFAA publishes a textbook called *Fitness: Theory and Practice*. It costs about $40. Independent providers also offer training to prepare candidates for the AFAA exams. Prices for training courses vary widely, but anywhere from $300 to $400 is common.

Certification is generally good for two years, after which instructors must become recertified. Recertification is accomplished by attending continuing education classes. The AFAA periodically provides certification reviews, workshops, and instructor training courses. You will find contact information for the AFAA and many other certifying organizations in the back of this book.

In general, these programs all cover the same material. Preparation for any of the major certifying bodies' exams requires an understanding of the fundamentals of the exercise sciences: anatomy, kinesiology, and physiology. You will also need to know the standards and guidelines for exercise for different populations, such as children, adults, and the elderly. You can expect to train in the fields of aerobic conditioning, health, fitness, nutrition, weight management, and lifestyle management. You will also gain experience in group exercise instruction for teaching safe, enjoyable, motivating, and effective aerobic classes. Courses will also cover practical applications of fitness instruction, including program design, use of music, choreography, leadership, and communication skills. In addition, you will be expected to become familiar with the latest research and trends in the fitness industry.

SALARY RANGE

According to IDEA's Fifth Annual Fitness Industry Compensation Survey, in which information was obtained from more than 160 U.S., Canadian, and Puerto

Rican fitness facilities, aerobics instructors can expect to make between $16 and $18 per hour. The IDEA survey also recorded that "a significant portion of qualifying fitness industry professionals were offered paid sick and vacation time, health insurance, club membership and pro shop discounts."

IDEA is a membership organization for health and fitness professionals, with members in more than seventy different countries around the world. IDEA's mandate is to provide health and fitness professionals worldwide with credible information, continuing education, and career development resources. (You will find contact information for IDEA in the back of this book.)

According to Payscale.com, aerobics instructors can expect a salary range from $12 to $28 an hour. The sidebar above includes the most recent survey information at the time of publication. In general, the people with the most experience and education are paid the most.

Pay Scale Survey

Median Hourly Rate in the United States:	$13
Median Hourly Rates in Selected States:	
California	$18
Massachusetts	$12
New Jersey	$12
New York	$15
Ohio	$9
Pennsylvania	$10
Texas	$12
Washington	$11

CAREER PATH

While you're in high school, concentrate on classes that will help you prepare to become a certified aerobics instructor. Some courses you may want to take are physical education, health, biology, English, mathematics, and business. Join an aerobics class and get some real experience. This is a good way to see if you really are excited about a fitness career, and it is also a fun way to get into shape. Research the certifying agencies listed in

Summary

Job Description
Aerobics instructors conduct group exercise sessions that involve aerobic exercise, stretching, and muscle conditioning.

Necessary Education
May vary; generally need certifications in aerobics, cardiopulmonary resuscitation (CPR), and first aid.

Helpful High School Courses
Physical education, health, biology, English, mathematics, and business courses.

the back of this book and find one that suits you.

Once you've become a certified aerobics instructor, continue your education. Become certified in other fitness areas that interest you. Some aerobic instructors become group fitness instructors, personal trainers, wellness coaches, or pursue any of the other certified careers in the fitness field: these are covered in each of the following chapters of this book. If you have multiple certifications, your employment possibilities will expand.

Once you have experience in designing, coordinating, and managing exercise classes, you may have the opportunity to become an aerobics director at a health club or at the employee fitness center of a large corporation. This is an ideal way for an aerobics instructor to advance into management. However, keep in mind that a college education and managerial skills are needed to advance to supervisory or managerial positions.

CHAPTER 2

GROUP FITNESS INSTRUCTOR

G roup fitness instructors can be defined as aerobics instructors of years past who have evolved. For example, aside from aerobics, group fitness instructors are qualified to teach many different kinds of exercise in group settings. Group fitness is a popular career choice because your knowledge of multiple fitness training styles makes you more attractive to employers. As well, this option gives you the choice of teaching whatever kind of class interests you the most. Some of the choices include:

- **High/Low aerobics:** A great cardio workout combining high- and low-impact aerobics. It often includes conditioning with weights, body bars, and elastic bands.

- **Kickboxing:** Individual moves or partner work that provides a cardio workout.

- **Pilates:** A conditioning program that improves muscle control, flexibility, coordination, strength, and tone.

An innovative system of body/mind conditioning that was developed from the principles of Joseph Pilates.

- **Step aerobics:** A workout using an adjustable platform that is alternately stepped onto and then off from.
- **Strength training:** A workout that uses the body's response to working muscles more than they are accustomed to through resistance training. The muscles respond by becoming stronger.
- **Water aerobics:** A workout in a swimming pool that makes use of the natural resistance and support of water with aerobic movements.
- **Yoga:** A conditioning workout that features relaxation, stress reduction, strength improvement, flexibility, and stamina.

The American Council on Exercise's (ACE) group fitness instructor certification, for example, is for individuals providing any form of group instruction. The curriculum covers effective communication, instructional techniques, and motivational skills. Candidates who successfully pass the certification exam will have demonstrated their knowledge in areas such as:

- Exercise science
- Exercise programming
- Instructional techniques
- Professional responsibility

Specific examples of educational program content with definitions are included in the certification section of this chapter. In general, you must be very passionate about exercising and believe in its benefits if you want to become a group fitness instructor. You must have an outgoing personality, good communication and leadership skills, and a passion for performing. Most of all, you must really enjoy meeting people and be excited about helping them enjoy working out. If these traits are part of your personality, you are probably a good candidate for becoming a group fitness instructor.

WORK ENVIRONMENT

As a certified group fitness instructor, you can expect to work mostly indoors at a fitness club or gym. However, outdoor group activities are certainly possible. There is no reason why classes such as aerobics, kickboxing, or yoga couldn't be conducted outside. The pool where you teach water aerobics may also be outside.

If you work for yourself, you will set your own schedule and decide how many hours to put in each week. Full-time group fitness instructors earn enough to make a modest living. Since fitness centers are springing up in every region of the United States and Canada (and many other places around the world), and because fitness is becoming more popular, you will also be able to decide where you want to work. For example, if you work as an employee at a fitness center:

- You may receive a free membership to the facility.
- You may receive employee benefits, such as paid vacations, health insurance, discounts on nutritional supplements and workout apparel, or discounted membership to facilities in other locations.
- You may be encouraged to sell club memberships and in return, you may receive additional commissions.
- You may get bonuses for selling workout apparel or nutritional products.

When you are just getting started, you may find it necessary to work very early in the morning and sometimes late into the night. Work schedules can also require work on weekends—even on holidays. Usually the most experienced fitness workers get the best hours.

CERTIFICATION

Expectations for group fitness professionals are increasing. They are expected to teach much more than aerobics. Today's instructors are expected to include current trends in group exercise, such as kickboxing, dance forms, water fitness, mind/body classes, group strength training, and sports-specific classes, such as conditioning for tennis or conditioning for snow skiing. To be competitive in today's job market, one must become certified by passing an exam administered by an organization such as the American Council on Exercise (ACE) or the American Fitness Professionals and Associates (AFPA).

In the United States, the ACE is one of only two certifying agencies that are granted accreditation for all of their certification programs. This accreditation comes from the National Commission for Certifying Agencies (NCCA). The NCCA is the accreditation body of the National Organization for Competency Assurance (NOCA). The NCCA accreditation serves as the standard on how organizations should carry out certification. In Canada, a good place to start is your provincial fitness association or the Canadian Association of Fitness Professionals (Can-Fit-Pro). Many other organizations provide certifications as well. Normal eligibility requirements for certification are:

- You must be at least eighteen years of age.
- You must have a current adult CPR certification.
- Candidates are strongly encouraged to have a minimum level (approximately 100 hours) of practical experience in the health and fitness field.
- A first aid certification is recommended.

The ACE certification exam for group fitness instructor certification consists of 150 written multiple-choice questions covering exercise science, exercise programming, instructional techniques, and professional responsibility.

Exercise science makes up 21 percent of the questions and includes questions about:

- Basic physiology, anatomy, and kinesiology
- Correct training techniques
- Basic fitness testing terminology and testing procedures
- Physiological and anatomical considerations for special populations, such as the elderly or those who are physically or mentally disadvantaged
- Basic psychological issues affecting adherence, which is the degree to which an individual follows a prescribed program; for example, the amount of activity engaged in during a specified time period compared to the amount of activity recommended for that time period
- Basic nutrition and weight management

Exercise programming makes up 25 percent of the questions and includes questions about:

- Components of fitness classes
- Designing group exercise classes
- Modifications and adaptations of fitness programs for special populations, such as the elderly, children, or those who are physically disabled

Instructional techniques makes up 35 percent of the questions and include questions about:

- Techniques for monitoring exercise intensity
- Teaching strategies to modify incorrect movements
- Correct cueing. Cueing is the way an instructor efficiently communicates changes in exercise patterns to an exercise class. This keeps the flow of the class moving smoothly from start to finish.

- Teaching methodologies
- Injury prevention
- Emergency procedures: first aid, CPR

Professional responsibility makes up 19 percent of the questions and includes questions about:

- Current legal principles and issues as they relate to the responsibilities of a professional fitness instructor
- ACE Code of Ethics
- Accepted business standards and practices, such as understanding the difference between an employee and an independent contractor
- Emergency procedures: first aid, CPR, evacuation plans
- Insurance needs related to group exercise instruction

SAMPLE QUESTIONS FROM THE ACE GROUP FITNESS INSTRUCTOR CERTIFICATION EXAM SAMPLE TEST

1. Static Stretching invokes stretch reflex inhibition by stimulating the:
   a. myosin myofilament
   b. golgi tendion organ
   c. motor end plate
   d. saromere
19. Participation in regular physical activity can be advantageous for Type 2 diabetic since regular exercise:
   a. increases insulin secretion by the pancreas
   b. helps to stimulate muscle development
   c. aids in the maintenance of hyperglycemia
   d. increases sensitivity of the cells to insulin
23. What are the by-products of anaerobic activity?
   a. beta-endorphin and lactic acid
   b. lactic acid and ATP

c. carbon dioxide and water
d. carbon monoxide and oxygen
Answers:1. b., 19. d., 23. b.
Courtesy of http://www.acefitness.org

As a comparison, the American Fitness Professionals and Associates (AFPA) program for certified fitness aerobic instructors, which is the equivalent to the ACE group fitness instructor program, is designed to prepare participants to teach safe and effective group exercise programs through the development of leadership and technical skills. Topics covered are anatomy, physiology, kinesiology, care and prevention of aerobic injuries, aerobic class design, structure and workout combinations, body sculpting and resistance training with weights and tubing, and leadership skills. This course is designed for group fitness instructors who may teach aerobics, step, and muscle conditioning classes. AFPA topics covered include:

• Review of anatomy, kinesiology, and muscle physiology
• Injury prevention, identification, and treatment
• Choreography principles and leadership skills
• Use of music, choreography, and cueing
• Challenging resistance training, and cueing
• Class design circuits, interval-adding variety
• Sculpting and conditioning exercises
• Use of equipment such as tubing, bands, and balls

The AFPA advises applicants to plan for up to three months to complete their self-paced, self-study certification course. A score of 90 percent is required to pass the exam.

For comparison's sake, Carrie Donmoyer of the Aerobics and Fitness Association of America kindly provided the sample test questions on the next page. As you can see, program content is very similar.

AFAA's Primary Group Exercise Certification Sample Test Questions

1. Which of the following is an example of a basic exercise position?
   A. Supine
   B. Prone
   C. Seated
   D. All of the above

2. Which type of muscle contraction does NOT require the muscle to change length when exerted against a fixed resistance?
   A. Concentric
   B. Eccentric
   C. Isokinetic
   D. Isometric

3. Which of the following is NOT considered a method of muscular strength and muscular endurance training?
   A. Functional training
   B. Multimuscle, multijoint training
   C. Steady state training
   D. Torso stabilization training

4. What type of connective tissue connects bone to bone?
   A. Ligament
   B. Fascia
   C. Cartilage
   D. Tendon

5. If a student complains about pain that has been persistent over the past few weeks, a fitness instructor should:
   A. Recommend the student seek a health care provider's evaluation and treatment
   B. Try to evaluate the problem and make suggestions to the student
   C. Do nothing because some muscle pain is expected as a result of exercise
   D. Tell the student to ice the painful area after exercise and not to worry

SALARY RANGE

According to IDEA's Fifth Annual Fitness Industry Compensation Survey, group fitness instructors made an average hourly rate of $16 in 1999 and an average rate of $18 in 2000.

Club Industry, a business magazine for health and fitness facility management, listed similar average earnings for 1999 and 2000. The following is the main criteria for pay scale: degree/certification (63 percent), years of experience (54 percent), and continuing education (51 percent).

Summary

Job Description
Group fitness instructors conduct group exercise sessions that involve aerobic exercise, stretching, and muscle conditioning. They often teach in classroom settings.

Necessary Education
May vary; generally need a group fitness instructor certification, and certifications in CPR and first aid.

Helpful High School Courses
Physical education, health, biology, English, mathematics, and business courses.

According to the American Council on Exercise 2003 Salary Survey, a full-time group fitness instructor (forty hours per week) can expect to make between $20,000 and $25,000 per year. The average hourly rate is $20.66. As a full-time group fitness instructor working for a company, one can expect health, dental, and life insurance; paid vacations; and sick pay. There are no benefits for group fitness instructors who are self-employed.

According to the Web site Payscale.com, which provides real-time salary survey information, the median income for a fitness trainer or aerobics instructor in the United States is $26,327 at the time of publication.

Information available on Exercisejobs.com indicates that fitness instructors make from $10 to $29 per hour.

CAREER PATH

While you are in high school, concentrate on classes that will help you train to become a group fitness instructor. Some classes you may want to take include physical education, health, biology, English, mathematics, and business. You'll often need to be certified in CPR and first aid before you qualify to take fitness certification courses. Accordingly, it is a good idea to go ahead and get your CPR and first aid certificates while you're in high school. There is information in the back of this book about whom to contact regarding these certifications.

You may also join a health club or gym and get some instruction in weight training and cardiovascular fitness from a certified fitness worker. Ask the instructor questions and be willing to listen. This person could become a valuable adviser as you strive to become a professional fitness worker.

Research the certifying agencies listed in the back of this book to find one that suits you. Once you've become a certified group fitness instructor, continue your education. Become certified in other areas of fitness that interest you. You could also become a personal trainer, wellness coach, or any of the other certified careers in the fitness fields covered in the following chapters. If you have multiple certifications, your employment possibilities will expand and your salary will go up. If you want to work your way into a management position, a college education is usually necessary.

Most positions require a bachelor's degree in an exercise field. Experience in the field and viable certification might allow you to move into this position without a degree. An entry-level position in a club or an organization with career growth opportunities can be ideal for learning the business and moving into the management position of fitness director.

CHAPTER 3

PERSONAL TRAINER

Many of those who make it their business to track trends in the fitness industry consider personal training to be one of the fastest-growing industries in North America. The government statistics included elsewhere in this book support this idea. It's easy to see why. Look around you. Obesity is at epidemic levels. Watch the news. You'll hear about excessive medical and health care costs. Those expenses are skyrocketing because many people know little or nothing about how to get started in a workout program. Often, they know even less about nutrition.

According to *The Canadian Physical Activity, Fitness, & Lifestyle Approach*, which was published in 2003, about 20 percent of people in North America are committed to working out. A whopping 60 percent know they should work out but haven't made the commitment to exercise. Another 20 percent simply don't care. With the right training—including behavior modification techniques—you can help people to become fit and stay that way.

The Mind/Body Connection

Many people suffer unnecessarily through the symptoms of disease. Often all that is necessary to live a healthier life is regular exercise. Unfortunately, this is easier said than done. Much of the reasons are psychological. Personal trainers can help people make regular workouts a part of their lives by knowing how to address the mind/body connection. Regular exercise can lessen the symptoms of (or can often cure) the following chronic diseases.

Cardiovascular disease: Cardiovascular disease is the leading cause of death in the United States, killing more than 700,000 people annually. A heart attack occurs every twenty-five seconds, and the average male has a 50 percent chance of dying from heart disease. A sedentary lifestyle is the most common risk factor for cardiovascular disease. Harvard researchers examined 10,269 men in 1962, 1966, and 1977, and found that those participating in sports had a lower risk of death from heart disease by 41 percent.

Cancer: Cancer is the second-leading cause of death in the United States. More than 500,000 people die of cancer every year. One out of every four deaths is from cancer. A study in the *American Journal of Epidemiology* tracked 17,719 men for fifteen years, and those who exercised were 88 percent less likely to develop prostate cancer.

Decreased muscle mass: After age forty-five, many people lose muscle mass, and for every pound of muscle lost, the resting metabolic rate drops by nearly fifty calories a day. Increased muscle mass increases the amount of calories you burn and helps prevent obesity.

Diabetes: An estimated 16 million people in the United States have diabetes mellitus—half of whom do not know it (because they are asymptomatic) and are not being treated for the disease. Every year, approximately 798,000 people are diagnosed with diabetes. About 50,000 deaths occur annually. An eight-year study of thirty-four- to fifty-nine-year-old women showed that women who exercised vigorously at least once a week had a one-third lower risk of adult-onset diabetes than sedentary women or those who exercised less frequently.

High blood pressure: Twenty-five percent of the adult population has high blood pressure, and 25 percent are in the near-high range. The death rate from high blood pressure is about 9,200 deaths a year (in the United States). Several studies have shown that exercise can reduce high blood pressure for some people.

Memory loss: By forty-five years of age, impulses between neurons in the brain can begin to slow by as much as 20 percent. A study found that middle-aged adults who improved their fitness by 15 percent through cycling also raised their scores on a memory test.

Obesity: One-third of Americans are overweight. This is an 8-percent increase since 1976.

Osteoarthritis: A study found that overweight middle-aged and older women could cut their risk of osteoarthritis of the knees in half by losing eleven pounds (five kilograms) over ten years. The same risk loss is assumed for men.

Osteoporosis: Because of the prevalence of osteoporosis in women, one out of every thirteen women over thirty-five years old will eventually fracture a hip due to a fall or accident. Studies have shown that bones respond well to resistance training with weights by increasing density.

Stroke: Strokes kill about 144,000 people annually and are the third-leading cause of death (in the United States). A study in the *British Medical Journal*—with 125 first-time stroke patients and 198 people as a healthy control group—found that subjects aged fifteen to twenty-five who exercised had a 76 percent lower risk of having a stroke. Those between ages twenty-five and forty had a 57 percent lower risk, and forty- to fifty-five-year-olds had a 37 percent reduction.

Source: http://www.FitnessManagement.com

At the same time, the baby boomers (a large group of people in our population born roughly between 1945 and 1960) are aging and they don't like it. They're doing everything they can to find the fountain of youth—and the best place to find it is through the guidance of a certified personal trainer. Personal trainers are likely to become more and more important as people begin to realize that prevention is the key to maintaining good health.

What does it take to be a personal trainer? Personal trainers must have a sound understanding of the functions and vital processes of the human body in order to effectively design personalized nutrition and physical fitness training programs. Personal trainers will benefit from becoming knowledgeable about special population groups such as seniors, children, pregnant women, and the physically challenged. This is because such knowledge will provide a personal trainer with more opportunities to obtain new clients. It is essential that good personal trainers be full of energy, have the ability to motivate, and are conscious of safety. In addition, like any entrepreneur, a personal trainer must understand marketing, networking, and public relations in order to attract clients.

WORK ENVIRONMENT

Once certified, personal trainers can start a personal training business from their own homes. They can train in a client's home gym, at community recreation centers, hospital fitness facilities, universities and local colleges, health clubs, gyms, the YMCA, and the YWCA. As a personal trainer working for yourself:

- You can work at home, in a client's home, or at a facility.
- You create your own work schedule.
- You make all the business decisions.
- You are responsible for making your own quarterly tax payments.
- The facility you work in will have extensive equipment.
- You may receive a free membership to the facility.
- You may be required to give a percentage of your money to the club or pay a rental fee.
- You may receive benefits if you become an employee instead of an independent contractor.
- Management personnel will assign you clients.
- You may receive a commission for selling memberships and nutritional products.

CERTIFICATION

To become a certified personal trainer, you must go through one of several certification programs offered by many organizations, such as the National Strength and Conditioning Association or the American College of Sports Medicine. You can find a list of certifying organizations in the United States and Canada in the back of this book. Canadians may want to start with the Canadian Society for Exercise Physiology (CSEP) or the Canadian Association of Fitness Professionals (Can-Fit-Pro).

Though there are some differences, certifying agencies cover the same educational content and require similar eligibility requirements. For specific requirements and subject matter, contact the certifying agencies for more information.

To give you an idea of what to expect, here are some of the typical eligibility requirements for taking a certification exam:

- You must be at least eighteen years of age.
- You must hold a current adult CPR certification.
- A first aid certification may be required or is strongly suggested.
- Candidates are strongly encouraged to have a minimum level (approximately 100 hours) of practical experience in the health and fitness field.

The American Council on Exercise Personal Trainer Certification Exam consists of 150 written multiple-choice questions covering the following areas of study:

Client assessment, covering 20 percent of the questions, includes questions about:

- Obtaining health/medical information.
- Obtaining a detailed lifestyle and exercise history.

- Assessing client expectations, preferences (weight loss, building muscle mass, creating muscle definition, better cardiovascular fitness, and more energy), motivation, and readiness.

- Conducting appropriate baseline measurements. For instance, what is the client's resting heartbeat? What is the client's starting ratio between fat and muscle content? How agile is the client? Baseline measurements are necessary for accurately judging a client's progress.

Program design, covering 21 percent of the questions, includes questions about:

- Interpreting the results of the client assessment. What kind of workout program would be best suited to the client?

- Establishing client-specific fitness goals and ways to objectively measure client progress.

- Determining appropriate fitness parameters based on client assessment.

- Addressing health risk factors for the client.

Program implementation and adjustment, covering 29 percent of the questions, includes questions about:

- Teaching safe and effective exercise techniques.

- Teaching lifestyle strategies that promote physical activity.

- Making appropriate program modifications based on continuing client assessments and feedback.

- Promoting exercise adherence—in other words, motivating the client to achieve short-term goals during workouts.

Applied sciences, covering 15 percent of the questions, includes questions about:

- Exercise physiology—how exercise impacts the vital processes and mechanisms in the body
- Kinesiology and elementary biomechanics
- Anatomy
- Motor learning/control
- Nutrition and healthy eating
- Substance use and abuse
- Weight management
- Stress management
- Basic behavioral sciences

One's professional role is covered by another 15 percent of the questions. This includes questions about:

- Emergency policy, plans, and procedure.
- Scope of practice—in other words, what falls within the range of personal training? What falls outside the range? How do you handle medical questions that come up during the course of working with a client?
- Legal responsibilities. This could include the health and well-being of your client within the scope of your practice, tax responsibilities of an independent contractor (versus an employee), and even copyright laws with regard to the music you use during client workouts.
- Ethical responsibilities. These may include making sure to work within the scope of your practice, client confidentiality, punctuality, and responsibility—in other words, being professional.
- Fair business practices. For example, a personal trainer should conduct himself or herself with honesty, integrity, forthrightness, and dignity. One

should encourage practices and conduct activities in a manner that positively reflects on the personal trainer as a member of the fitness industry. A personal trainer should act with competence and strive to maintain and improve his or her competence and that of others in the industry. A personal trainer should disclose all relevant information regarding the terms and conditions of a transaction or service which may affect the decisions of a client. A professional trainer should always regard all financial and other information supplied by the client as being strictly confidential.

Sample Questions from the ACE Personal Trainer Certification Exam Sample Test

1. Which rotator cuff muscle abducts the arm?
   a. Infraspinatus
   b. Supraspinatus
   c. Subscapularis
   d. Teres minor

8. When working with a physician-cleared client who is 70 years old with borderline hypertension, which of the following precautions should you take?
   a. Avoid the Valsalva maneuver and encourage isometric exercise
   b. Monitor blood pressure and avoid the Valsalva maneuver
   c. Encourage isometric exercise, monitor blood pressure, and avoid the Valsalva maneuver
   d. Lower resistance and increase repetitions, avoid the Valsalva maneuver, and monitor blood pressure

56. Although your client verbally agrees with your suggestions, you notice that throughout your discussion she sits with her arms crossed and her

eyes downcast. The BEST course of action is to:
a. Offer a detailed breakdown of the first month
b. Ask her how she feels about the program
c. Have her perform the exercises that you
   have described
d. Refer her to a qualified health professional

Answers: 1. b, 8. d, 56. b.
Courtesy of http://www.acefitness.org

For the sake of comparison, look at the American Fitness Professionals and Associates program for personal trainers, which covers the following information:

• Anatomy, kinesiology, and a review of muscle physiology
• Client assessment and screening
• Cardiovascular health
• Exercise program design
• Exercise programming for special populations
• Flexibility training
• Strength training: upper and lower body, core conditioning
• Business for personal trainers
• Injury prevention and first aid procedures
• Nutrition for the twenty-first century

Most certification programs take between three and six months—including study time and testing. Though it is not necessary, for the maximum employability—in addition to the certification program—one is also encouraged to obtain a bachelor's diploma or degree in a fitness-related field, such as exercise science, exercise physiology, sports medicine, physical education, biomechanics, or kinesiology.

SALARY RANGE

According to the ACE 2003 Salary Survey, full-time personal trainers (forty hours per week) made between $30,000 and $35,000 per year and an average of $37 per hour. Personal trainers employed at fitness facilities reported receiving typical benefits such as health care coverage, dental and life insurance, paid vacation, and sick pay. Independent contractors (those who are self-employed) are responsible for saving money to cover their medical insurance, tax responsibilities, and vacations.

According to the International Fitness Professionals Association (IFPA), the salary potential for personal trainers varies from $35 to more than $175 per hour! What is the difference between being a $35-an-hour trainer and a trainer who makes $175 per hour or more? The answer is hard work, dedication, a willingness to learn, and constantly striving for excellence. The IFPA Web site says it all in a slogan: "Success is a journey—not a destination!"

CAREER PATH

Begin by studying physical education, health, biology, English, mathematics, and business courses while you're in high school. Plan on earning a college degree in a fitness-related field. Explore certification options. You'll need to gain credentials through a respected organization. There is a list of certifying agencies in the back of this book. It is a good idea to speak with existing trainers. They can offer insight into the realities of the profession.

If you want to work for yourself, start thinking about a plan for marketing and attracting clientele. You may want to associate yourself with a few fitness centers that could benefit from having a personal trainer available. It's a good idea to build a network of friends, associates, and others—even medical professionals—who might offer a referral system for building a client base.

If you plan to work as an employee at a health club, you'll want to think about preparing a résumé and a business plan. You'll be meeting with health club owners who will want to know not only if you're a qualified personal trainer but, also, if you'll be a business asset. This could be a source of clients.

INTERVIEW WITH A PROFESSIONAL FITNESS AND LIFESTYLE CONSULTANT

Tony Armstrong is certified as a professional fitness and lifestyle consultant through the Canadian Society for Exercise Physiology. This is one of the higher levels of certification for personal trainers. Tony had to complete postsecondary education to obtain this title.

Because of his level of education, the scope of his practice is very broad. It ranges from working with apparently healthy clients, to working with special populations, to assessing and advising elite athletes. Tony is qualified to do just about any kind of fitness assessment. His certification also allows him to do occupational testing for firefighters. The following questions and answers are from the author's interview with Tony:

How long have you been working in the fitness field?
In excess of twenty years.

What interested you about the fitness field?
I had always been interested in sports and it seemed like a natural progression when looking into post-secondary education.

How did you get into the fitness field?
I attended George Brown College [in Toronto] in 1983, and in my final semester, I completed my placement at a fitness

Summary

Job Description
Personal trainers guide and motivate clients to reach their peak fitness potential by developing customized fitness plans based on an assessment of their clients' fitness needs.

Necessary Education
Personal trainers need at least a personal trainer certification from a nationally recognized agency, as well as certifications in CPR and first aid.

Helpful High School Courses
Physical education, health, biology, English, mathematics, and business courses.

center in Toronto. At that point in time, I began personal training and realized that this career path was a perfect fit for me. The fitness field allows you to diversify and not be pigeonholed into one mundane job.

What do you like most about what you do?
Interacting with individuals that have various health-related objectives and helping people realize goals that they never thought were possible.

What is the most challenging thing about what you do?
This is not only a job about fitness, but a profession based upon people. Consequently, just because I provide them with an excellent program, certainly it doesn't mean that they will adhere to it. It's very frustrating when clients don't take ownership of their own destiny. As well, it's hard to be always positive and upbeat, which are key to being a successful fitness/personal trainer.

Tony also commented:
This is definitely not a nine-to-five job. The hours can be extremely long, as you have to work around an individual's schedule. The vast majority of people in the fitness field are not making large salaries and therefore many choose an alternative career path.

CHAPTER 4

CERTIFIED AQUATICS INSTRUCTOR

A quatic fitness is not swimming laps, nor is it synchronized swimming or water ballet. As a matter of fact, no swimming at all is involved. Aquatic fitness workouts are upright exercises that are done in the water.

You can choose from two types of upright water workouts. "Water walking" is a good starting point for people who are out of shape or recovering from surgery. This form is also good for people with chronic physical or motor skill disabilities, such as arthritis, multiple sclerosis (MS), amyotrophic lateral sclerosis (ALS), commonly known in the United States as Lou Gehrig's disease. Water walking works well for increased flexibility, balance, strength, and general well-being.

If you also want to increase your cardiovascular fitness, water aerobics, or an "aqua fitness" class, is right for you. A water aerobic workout consists of standing in water that is rib- to chest-deep and (for example) jogging, bicycling, boxing, or cross-country skiing. These are all traditional forms of aerobic exercise. Water has approximately twelve times the resistance of air. When you're performing jumping jacks in the water, this extra resistance requires more muscular effort and strength. For example, try at least twenty minutes of mixing jumping jacks, lunges, jumps, knee lifts, and deep-water (suspended) moves to see how the natural resistance of water maximizes the effects of these traditional dry land exercises.

Water, of course, also decreases the effect of gravity on the body. Since you are more buoyant in the water, less of your body weight hits the ground. For example, when you're in chest-deep water, only 25 percent of your normal body weight affects your ankle, knee, and hip joints. For people with joint problems, aqua fitness is a great way to work muscles, gain cardiovascular fitness, and have a great time.

There are many job opportunities for careers in aqua fitness. Certification is offered in areas such as aquatics instruction, aquatic personal training, aquatic kickboxing, aquatic senior fitness, and aquatics for special populations (such as people with arthritis, asthma, and multiple sclerosis).

WORK ENVIRONMENT

Obviously, fitness workers in aquatic fitness will find themselves working in or near swimming pools most of the time. To name a few examples, those swimming pools may be at a health club or YMCA, in a senior center, or at a resort. If working in a swimsuit sounds better to you than working in a business suit, this may be the best environment for you. On the other hand, if you're worried about looking like a wrinkled prune from being in the water all day or about the effect that chlorinated water will have on your eyes and hair, then maybe one of the other fitness careers would be a better choice for you.

CERTIFICATION

There are many certification programs for aqua fitness workers. For example, the American Fitness Professionals and Associates (AFPA) offers an Aquatics Instructor Home Study Certification. Its contents include:

- Designing challenging and effective aquatic fitness classes
- Designing resistance training techniques for aquatics
- Reviewing hydrodynamics
- Designing modifications for special populations
- Injury prevention
- Designing interval and circuit-training techniques for aquatics
- Reviewing anatomy, kinesiology, and muscle physiology for pool safety
- Teaching on deck and in the water

The AFPA recommends allowing up to three months to complete the certification course, which is self-paced.

Aquatic Alliance International (AAI) offers an Aquatic Fitness Instructor Certification. This program includes six hours of pool time and six hours of classroom time. It usually is held over a two-day period. Class content covers theoretical and practical principles as well as skills necessary to get started in the water fitness industry. Participants are able to practice aquatic moves and formats including water walking and deepwater exercise. Emphasis is on practical application.

The certification is effective for two years. Prerequisites are CPR and first aid certificates.

The Aquatics Fitness Professionals Association International (A-PAI) is a national aqua aerobics certification organization that provides certifications in water aerobics (core certification), aquatic personal training, aquatic kickboxing, and senior fitness. It also offers more than thirty water aerobics workshops and five land workshops in kickboxing, pilates, toning, and step aerobics. A-PAI workshops are approved for AEA, ACE, and AFAA continuing education credits.

The Aquatic Exercise Association (AEA) offers a fitness instructor certification and a personal training certification. The aquatic fitness instructor certification class content covers the following general categories:

- Exercise anatomy
- Exercise physiology
- Movement analysis: applied anatomy
- Physical fitness
- Physical laws/aquatic equipment
- Health screening/injury prevention/special populations
- Aquatic environment/leadership and programming/choreography
- Nutrition/weight management
- Related knowledge: exercise behavior/legal issues

Prerequisites: All certifications require proof of current and valid CPR certification. For the aquatic personal trainer certification, you should obtain the AEA's aquatic fitness instructor certification, first aid and sports safety/injury training, as well as basic water rescue skills. The AEA is an approved continuing education provider for ACE, AEA, AFAA, ATRIC, and NATA-BOC.

Sample Test Questions for the AEA Aquatic Fitness Instructor Certification

1. Water exercise participants often notice that their recovery heart rates:
   a. are much higher than with land based aerobics
   b. show signs of arrhythmia
   c. are attained more quickly than in land based aerobics
   d. remain elevated for a 10-second pulse rate check
2. Which metabolic pathway is primarily utilized for short bursts of energy or for the initial stages of longer duration activity?
   a. Kreb's cycle
   b. fatty acid oxidation
   c. ATP-PC system
   d. aerobic system
3. The relationship between heart rate and oxygen consumption differences in the water may be a result of all the following factors except:
   a. reduced drag
   b. gravity
   c. increased compression
   d. the dive reflex
4. Which piece of equipment is designed specifically to utilize drag as the primary resistance?
   a. elastic bands
   b. foam dumbbells
   c. water-filled dumbbells
   d. webbed gloves
5. Which muscle is responsible for flexion of the knee?
   a. vastus medialis
   b. latissimus dorsi
   c. biceps brachii
   d. biceps femoris
6. Flexing and extending from the shoulder under water works which muscle groups?
   a. medial deltoid and rhomboids
   b. anterior deltoid and posterior deltoid
   c. middle trapezius and pectoralis
   d. upper trapezius and deltoids

7. Cueing a jumping jack in threes, with a "Single, Single, Double" would be an example of which type of cueing?

a directional

b. numerical

c. rhythmic

d. tep

8. Which tempo kick does the following chart represent?

Music Beat	1	2	3	4	5	6	7	8
	Right Kick	Left Kick	Right Kick	Left Kick	Right Kick	Left Kick	Right Kick	Left Kick

a. land tempo

b. water tempo

c. 1/2 water tempo

9. A deconditioned student begins exercising daily for 1 hour or more and soon experiences overuse injury. The principle of _____ was ignored.

a. variability

b. progressive overload

c. specificity

d. adaptation

10. Explosive moves such as tuck jumps increase intensity because of:

a. acceleration

b. inertia

c. buoyancy

d. frontal area

11. Muscular strength is BEST obtained through:

a. isometric exercises done several times per week

b. repetitive action over a long duration

c. moderate weight with several repetitions over time

d. few repetitions with heavy weights

12. This is "the immediate energy source" of a muscle cell:

a. CP

b. oxygen

c. glycogen

d. ATP

13. **The law of levers can be utilized to:**
    a increase intensity
    b. decrease intensity
    c. increase and decrease intensity
    d. none of the above
14. **When you add weighted equipment to a standing arm curl (elbow flexion and extension) in the water, you are:**
    a. toning the biceps
    b. toning the triceps
    c. toning the biceps and triceps
    d. toning the deltoids and latissimus
15. **"Press your heels to the pool bottom" is an example of which type of cue?**
    a. motivational
    b. form
    c. transitional
    d. directional

WaterARTTM Fitness Inc., which is based in Ontario, Canada, and which has offices in Miami, Florida, offers the following certifications:

• **Fundamentals instructor certification:** During this core course, you will review current research in water fitness and examine basic principles of exercise science so that you may apply these principles to aquatic training. You will learn the properties of water and experience the difference between land and water exercise design to discover that water training is unique. By the end of the program, you will understand how to design a multilevel shallow water class using the basic water moves and variations and working positions that help you to vary impact and intensity so participants can work at their personal best.
Prerequisite: You must be at least sixteen years old. This program is worth 12.5 AFAA credits and 10.0

ACE and other certifying organization continuing education credits.

- **Personal trainer specialist certification:** You will learn how to design individual programs for a variety of levels including post rehabilitation and athletic training. This course will detail how to establish an appropriate program based on health history and lifestyle questionnaires, a thorough physical assessment, and comprehensive goal-setting techniques that will aid in the planning of a result-oriented program. You will experience a complete exercise inventory utilizing a variety of equipment and techniques so that you may build your career toolbox.
  Prerequisites: You must be a veteran in the field and/or have completed WaterARTTM Fundamental Certification (or equivalent). This program is worth 10.0 AFAA credits and 1.6 ACE and other certifying organization continuing education credits.

WaterARTTM offers other programs as well, such as rehabilitation specialist certification and weight management certification.

SALARY RANGE

According to the American Council on Exercise (ACE) 2003 Salary Survey Results, specialty instructors—such as those in the fields of aquatics, spinning, and kickboxing—made between $20,000 to $25,000 per year.

CAREER PATH

Begin by studying physical education, health, biology, English, mathematics, and business courses while you are in high school. It is a great idea to have a few years of experience on a swim team or water polo team. You must hold a current adult CPR certification before you can take most certification courses. Accordingly, you may as well get this certificate while you are in high school. A first aid certification may be required or strongly suggested. This is another certificate you can get while still in high school.

Explore certification options. You'll need to obtain credentials through a respected organization. There is a list of certifying agencies in the back of this book. It is a good idea to speak with experienced trainers. They can offer valuable insight into the current realities of the profession.

If you want to work for yourself, start thinking about a plan for marketing and attracting clientele. You may want to associate yourself with a few fitness centers equipped with swimming pools that could benefit from having a personal trainer available. It's a good idea to build a network of friends, associates, and others, (even medical professionals), who might offer a referral system which can be helpful for seeking clients.

If you plan to work as an employee at a health club with a swimming pool, you'll want to think about preparing a résumé and a business plan. You'll be meeting with health club owners and they'll want to know that

Summary

Job Description
Aquatics instructors guide and motivate clients to reach their peak fitness potential by leading exercise routines done in the water.

Necessary Education
Aquatics instructors need to have at least a professional aquatics instructor certification from a nationally recognized agency and certifications in CPR and first aid.

Helpful High School Courses
Physical education, health, biology, English, mathematics, and business courses, swim team, diving team and/or water polo.

you're not only a qualified aquatics trainer, but that you'll be a good asset for their business. This could be a source of clients.

CHAPTER 5

FITNESS MODEL

C ertification is not necessary to become a fitness model. However, that said, it's important to be aware that the path to becoming this kind of fitness professional is probably more difficult than many other careers in the fitness industry. Also, your chance of being a successful fitness model is less certain. All fitness models—male or female—must look like the fittest people in the world. While it may not be necessary to have mammoth muscles, both male and female fitness models need to have muscles that have been refined to the extent that their body fat ranges from no more than between 3 to 8 percent. These models set the standard for the fitness ideal. Ultimately, if you really want to become a fitness model, you need to be aware that there is a lot to learn and you'll have a lot of hard work ahead of you.

MAKING AN HONEST SELF-EVALUATION

Reality check number one: If there is one universal truth in the modeling business, it's that some people are very photogenic and some are not. Before you decide to try to become a fitness model, you'll need to be extremely honest with yourself.

Reality check number two: There are millions of great-looking young men and women out there. However, keep in mind that looks alone aren't going to make you a successful fitness model. You're going to have to hustle like everyone else who wants to make it in the industry.

Reality check number three: There is no single path toward becoming a successful fitness model. There is no magic secret—just a lot of study, and consistent hard work.

If you think you have the looks, ambition, and commitment that it will take, the rest of this chapter—which outlines some of the key things a person can do to greatly improve his or her chances of "making it" in the fitness business as a model—will be of great help to you.

Supporting Yourself While You're Getting Started

The truth is that very few people make a living as fitness models. It is also true that it will likely take you some time to create the body you want (and need) in order to break into the business. Therefore, a good strategy is to first become a fitness instructor. As you study for your certification, you'll also be learning what you need to shape and tone to achieve an appropriate physique. When you're certified, you'll be able to make money training others and be able to do your own workouts in the very same facilities. Working as a fitness instructor is also a great way to gain exposure for yourself, and a great way to network—which is a very important part of business success. There is more on networking in this chapter.

BODYBUILDING

There are many, many books, magazines, videos and Web sites out there that cover the best way to go about being a professional bodybuilder. There are also a lot of people who may claim that they know a quick route to becoming a bodybuilder. However, do not be surprised if they then take your money and run. In other words, be on the lookout for scam artists. The very best way to sculpt a physique that will be an asset in the fitness industry is to take the time to learn everything you need to know. There are no quick fixes. What follows is general advice for getting started.

- **Get a checkup:** Before taking up a strenuous activity, seek the approval of your family doctor.

- **Make the decision to change:** Changing bad habits and starting good ones is an essential part to becoming a bodybuilding success. You need to integrate physical fitness into your weekly routine—not just in order to lose some weight, and not just to tone up, but as a way to begin a new lifestyle. In your weekly workouts, make it a priority to clear one to one and a half hours per day, three days per week.

- **Find a gym or fitness center to join:** Most experts agree that it is better to train in a gym, as opposed to doing so in your home. The main reason is that unless you are very wealthy, you will be hard-pressed to access the quantity or quality of equipment and services that are found in gyms. Besides, working out is easier to do—not to mention, more enjoyable— when you are in a gym where you are surrounded by a variety of weights, machines, music, and people.

- **Start by working with a fitness trainer:** Usually, fitness centers and gyms will have a fitness trainer available who can help you establish a workout program. This program will be designed to help you achieve the results you want. Your trainer should also walk you through your fitness routine so that you can familiarize yourself with the equipment you'll be using. Also, he or she can instruct you in how to use the equipment properly in order to prevent possible injury.

- **Remember that for everyone, training is awkward in the beginning.** As time passes, you will become more familiar with the gym, the equipment, and your workout routine. Your confidence will increase. Just be positive and stick with it.

- **Don't be too serious.** Have some fun. Enjoy meeting new people at the gym. If you're going to become a fitness model, you'll need good social skills. Gyms and fitness clubs are a great place to network. The fitness business is a people business. Besides, if your workouts aren't enjoyable, you'll never keep it up long enough to succeed.

- **If you are thinking of taking steroids, DON'T.** If you use steroids, you will damage your health sooner or later. If you want to be a competitive bodybuilder, there are many events in which natural bodybuilders can compete.

- **Accept the facts about building muscles and losing body fat.** It's hard work. Reshaping your body and learning how your body responds to a different diet takes time. An appropriately shaped and toned body is not created overnight, but rather, it is formed over a period of years.

- **You're probably going to need to change your diet.** A great-looking body does not just mean large muscles. It also means having a healthy ratio of muscle versus body fat. All of those fabulous muscles you're building won't show under a layer of fat. That means eating sensibly and doing regular cardiovascular exercise. What is eating sensibly? Forget fast food. Some of the most common diet changes include drinking more water and limiting salt and excess calories. Emphasize fruit, vegetables, and whole grains in your diet and eat some lean meat or fish as well.

- **Visualize yourself succeeding.** Literally picture yourself with a more muscular and leaner body. When you want to stay home and eat a pizza instead of doing your workout, remember this image.
- **Sleep.** Everyone needs to sleep, but especially someone who is working toward building a better body. Our muscles repair and grow while we sleep.

If you follow these suggestions and take care of yourself, you will make amazing improvements to your body and overall health.

ACTING

If, by chance, you are contemplating a part-time or simultaneous acting career, keep in mind that this can aid you in developing speech and movement skills. In turn, you will be better prepared for in-front-of-the-camera action than would many other potential fitness models.

Acting may seem easy, but don't be fooled. It only looks so effortless due to the years actors spend perfecting their craft. There are many schools and classes that specialize in different branches of acting—for example, acting for stage, acting for commercials, special classes on improvisational acting, and other classes on voice training. As with bodybuilding, there are many people out there who will claim that they can lead you to the right path—however, there will be strings attached. For example, you may be asked to pay money up front. Again, be aware of scams. You'll need to be able to weed out good advice from bad, fact from fiction, truth from untruth.

A good place to begin your involvement in acting is by getting hands-on experience at your high school. This, or course, will be easier if there is a drama club. If not, look into beginning acting lessons at your local community college. This is a good and relatively inexpensive way to get some basic training. If it turns out that you love acting, your instructor will be able to provide you with good, sound advice on how to move forward with more advanced training.

MODELING

Unlike actors, models usually do not have to memorize lines and speak in front of rolling cameras. Also, you won't have to go through the nerve-wracking experience of performing a scene in front of numerous people you don't know. However, taking some professional modeling classes can give you a certain amount of poise and confidence that will help you in your interactions as a fitness model. As well, acting experience will give you an edge over other fitness models who have not honed these skills.

TAKE MODELING CLASSES

Modeling might seem easy, but it's not. It's a lot of hard work. There are some people for whom it's easier and more natural to pose in front of a camera than others. However, whether you're a natural or not, everyone who wants to be a professional model can benefit from starting with some basic instruction. Although casting agents will first consider your physical appearance, models with training and experience are the most sought after. Taking modeling classes from a professional school will give you the opportunity to improve your existing skills. It will also help you learn how to deal effectively with auditions.

As with acting schools, there are plenty of people out there who are waiting to take your money and run—or even worse. If you plan to take modeling lessons, be careful. Take some time to do your research. Make sure the modeling school has been around for a long time. You might want to check with the Better Business Bureau before signing up at a particular school. This will insure that you'll be giving your money to a bona fide business with a solid reputation.

PROFESSIONAL PORTFOLIOS AND ZED CARDS

Aside from gaining some basic instruction in acting or modeling, having a professional portfolio is another key element in terms of preparing yourself for a full-time modeling career.

THE BENEFITS OF A GOOD PORTFOLIO

Your portfolio should include a number of photos showing you in a variety of situations, or poses, as well as a current and well-written résumé. The key to a good portfolio is to select a well-established photographer who can capture your best features. Your résumé must include your current contact information, height, size, weight, measurements, previous training, and a history of your most recent work. Aside from actual looks, professionals will be hired according to versatility and the extent of prior modeling experience.

THE ZED CARD OR COMP CARD

Aside from your portfolio, the most important tool you'll have to market yourself is what is called a zed card or comp card (composite card). In most cases, these cards provide you with your one and only opportunity to make a good first impression. Zed or comp cards are usually 5 by 7 inches (12.7 by 17.8 centimeters). Normally, the front has a good headshot, or a full-body shot. The back will have anywhere from two to four good photos that should illustrate your versatility as a model. The zed will have contact information as well as your statistics and measurements. The printing and reproduction quality of these cards is extremely important. A shoddily produced card will make your photos look bad, which in the end will have a negative impact on you.

It will be your duty as an actor or model to mail out your zed or comp cards to agencies, casting directors, magazine editors, and production companies. However, it's important to keep in mind that this process can be quite costly and time-consuming. Most of the time, these cards will end up in a large file along with thousands of similar cards. However, if you're patient, thorough, and determined, you'll increase your chances of being sought after for work.

AGENCIES AND TALENT MANAGERS

At some point, you may need to select an agent or manager. You can do so by sending out a good photo (or head shot) and résumé to all the agents/managers in your area. They will call you back if they are impressed with your photo and are interested in representing you. Every major city has well-established talent agencies and management groups. Contact a few different agencies/managers and find out what their application requirements are. The key to success is retaining an agent/manager who is well-established and experienced. Be sure to ask for references and credentials before signing any contracts.

NETWORKING, MARKETING, AND BUSINESS

Once you've achieved the awesome body you've been working at perfecting, great social skills and poise, business cards, a portfolio, and the zed cards to go with it, you'll need to learn something about networking and marketing. If you don't network and market yourself properly, you can pretty much forget about having any real success as a fitness model. Fitness modeling isn't just about being in great shape, it's about being a smart businessperson with a positive attitude and great social skills.

Once you're out of school and on your way, you'll want to pick one or more major industry shows to attend every year, such as the following:

- Arnold Classic Fitness Weekend
- Can-Fit-Pro Convention
- Mr. Olympia
- The Emerald Cup
- TheFitExpo
- The IDEA World Fitness Convention

Luck is where opportunity meets preparedness. What does this mean? Never go to a show without professional-looking business cards and comp cards that you can give editors, publishers, photographers, and other industry insiders. Successful fitness models (or any independent fitness professional) are self-marketing machines. They can be found at any event or facility where they think there may be an opportunity to meet the right people.

The more industry insiders you meet, and the more cards you hand out, the greater chance you'll have of stumbling across the opportunities that can supercharge your career. Success means giving out hundreds of cards and taking home just as many from the people you come into contact with. Success means being organized and following up on each and every contact that you make. It should go without saying that you should be well rested, in good condition, and looking your best.

COMPETING

Do you need to compete if your goal is to be a successful fitness model? The answer is no. Competing is not a part of many well-known fitness models' success stories. Nonetheless, at the most prestigious bodybuilding competitions, editors, publishers, photographers, vitamin or health supplement company owners, and other business people will be interested in who does well in these competitions, not to mention who looks great. Their businesses depend upon seeking out winners who they think will help benefit their business. This means that competing can drastically improve your exposure.

It's Not What You Have, It's What You Do with It

However, you must realize that winning a show does not in any way guarantee success in terms of the business end of being a fitness model. Winning a title can be a stepping stone, but it is not in itself any guarantee of success in the industry. Think of it as the same thing as having a college degree. It's not the fact that you actually have one that will necessarily help you advance; more important is what you do with it. If you want to compete for the fun of it, then by all means go for it, but it is important to focus on competing as it relates to the overall business of being a fitness model.

WEB SITES

A professionally created Web site can be a very useful way to market yourself as a fitness professional. (Remember, you'll need a way to support yourself while you're getting into the fitness model business.) It's also a great way to show off your portfolio of professional head and body shots. A well-made and nicely designed Web site provides industry insiders with a quick, easy, and accessible way for them to seek you out and—if they like what they see—get in touch with you. You may also want to think about writing an advice column for your Web site that you frequently update. This is a surefire way to increase traffic to your site. More hits on your Web site translates to having a larger quantity of people looking at your photos. If you're a fitness instructor, it means more people considering you for their needs. Ultimately, a professionally created Web site is a great way to help establish your credentials as an expert.

WORKING REALITIES

Someday (after a lot of hard work and a dose of talent as well) you may actually become a bona fide, well-known fitness personality with your own line of merchandise (ranging from vitamin supplements, to exercise videos and DVDs, to a line of workout clothing or anything else that you can market as being good for your health and your body). You may even have producers calling your agent for movie roles. All dreaming aside, until any of this actually happens, your most likely source of employment will be as an equipment or product demonstrator or a product promoter or model. Demonstrators, product promoters, and models are essential in the industry as they are ultimately responsible for creating public interest in buying specific fitness clothing, health or exercise products, and other related services.

YOUR WORKING ENVIRONMENT

If you get a job as a demonstrator, you'll most likely find yourself in a store, shopping mall, or trade show. Fitness models may find themselves working anywhere from a comfortable, climate-controlled studio to a cold, damp outdoor location. Schedules can be demanding. The locations where you'll be working are selected based on both the nature of the audience and the type of product. You may also be employed to demonstrate and promote a product on a videotape, a DVD, on the Internet, or for a spot on television.

EDITORIAL, COMMERCIAL, AND CATALOG WORK

Keep in mind, however, that the majority of most modeling jobs are for printed publications. As such, models usually do a combination of editorial, commercial, and catalog work. Editorial print modeling uses still photographs of models for magazine covers or to accompany feature articles. However, it does not include modeling for advertisements. Commercial print modeling includes work for advertisements in magazines and newspapers, and for outdoor advertisements such as billboards. Catalog models appear in department store and mail order catalogs.

HIGHLY COVETED WORK IN TELEVISION

Fitness models may compete with actors and actresses for work in television. Television work includes commercials, cable television programs, and even game shows. Keep in mind that competition for this kind of work is very intense. This is because of the potential for high earnings and extensive exposure. It's also the result of there being far more talented actors than there are available acting jobs.

THE IMPORTANCE OF A GOOD AGENT

Almost all models work through agents. Agents provide a link between models and clients. Clients pay models, while the agency receives a portion of the model's earnings for its services. Top models can make a great deal of money, but their careers are usually very short. This is why some agencies also provide bookkeeping and billing services for models and may offer financial planning services as well.

FITNESS PRODUCT DEMONSTRATORS AND PRODUCT PROMOTERS

Demonstrators and product promoters may work long hours while standing or walking, with little opportunity to rest. Some of them frequently travel. Night and weekend work is often required. Demonstrator and product promoter jobs may be found in communities throughout the United States and Canada, but modeling jobs are mostly concentrated in New York, Miami, and Los Angeles (or for Canada, in Vancouver and Toronto). Models often travel to work in faraway cities and in foreign countries. Hence, if you don't like to travel, or you actually have a fear of flying, this might not be a good option for you.

JOB OUTLOOK

According to the U.S. Department of Labor Bureau of Labor Statistics, "Employment of demonstrators, product promoters, and models is expected to grow about as fast as the average for all occupations through 2011. Job openings should be plentiful for demonstrators and product promoters. New jobs should arise as firms devote a greater percentage of marketing budgets to product demonstration. Employment of demonstrators, product promoters, and models is affected by downturns in the business cycle. Many firms tend to reduce advertising budgets during recessions."

Those who wish to pursue a modeling career can expect a lot of competition for relatively few jobs. Ultimately, it's only fitness models who meet the unique requirements of the occupation (including superb looks, a great body, a charismatic personality, and savvy business skills) who will achieve regular employment. And one must keep in mind that even the best models can experience periods of unemployment.

SALARY RANGE

According to the U.S. Department of Labor Bureau of Labor Statistics, "Demonstrators and product promoters can expect to earn from between $8 and $20 an hour. Models earned between $6 and about $18 per hour. Earnings vary for different types of modeling, and pay also depends on the experience and reputation of the model. Earnings can be relatively high, particularly for

Summary

Job Description

Fitness models work as demonstrators in a variety of venues, and as models for various media including print, Internet, DVD, video, and film production.

Necessary Education

This requirement varies, but could include certification as a fitness instructor, acting lessons and/or modeling lessons.

Helpful High School Courses

People interested in becoming fitness models should have a well-rounded education, which includes physical education/sports, business, and public speaking and/or acting classes.

supermodels and others in high demand." Models occasionally receive clothing or clothing discounts instead of, or in addition to, regular earnings. Almost all models work with agents and pay 15 to 20 percent of their earnings in return for an agent's services. Models who do not find immediate work may receive payments, called advances, from their agents. An advance is very beneficial as it helps cover promotional costs and living expenses. Keep in mind that most models must provide their own health and retirement benefits.

CHAPTER 6

WELLNESS COACH

D octors, insurance companies, and legislators are beginning to understand that prevention is the best way to keep medical costs down. In the not-too-distant future, physicians may refer patients to wellness coaches along with prescribing medications to treat medical conditions that can be prevented, improved, or cured by exercise, nutrition, weight control, and stress management.

According to the Duke University Medical Center program for Executive Wellness Coaching, "Wellness Coaching is a form of consulting which focuses on assisting you to reach your goals, to examine how you approach problems and challenges in your life, and to embrace healthy lifestyle behaviors [in order] to achieve your optimal performance. A Wellness Coach assists and supports you in creating and sustaining physical and emotional wellness as you move through life."

Wellness coaching has its roots in applied behavioral science. Behavioral scientists have shown that one-on-one coaching is among the most effective approaches to helping people make and sustain improvements in their lives. More specifically, wellness coaches use behavior modification to help their clients achieve the results they desire. Behavior modification is a formalized process that promotes changes in behavior in a positive way.

Wellness coaching can be a career in itself, but in the context of fitness careers, it is often recognized by a certification that is added to group fitness instructor or personal trainer certifications. As a matter of fact, wellness coaching would be a valuable addition to any fitness worker's qualifications. While most fitness career certifications mainly focus on exercise, wellness coaching goes beyond the simple notion of exercise to deal with the whole client. This includes the body and the mind. In Canada, certified fitness consulting is a similar vocation requiring an education in many of the same subjects, including behavior modification.

The professional and yet personal (nonjudgmental) relationship between a wellness coach and client offers a profound level of support, guidance, and encouragement in terms of aiding and supporting a client in making lifestyle changes. A coach enables change by helping a client focus on a customized program based on a client's stated needs, values, vision, and goals. For example, a client's goal may be to attain a specific percentage of body fat. The client's vision may be a future self that is more energetic, resilient, and confident. The wellness coach will help the client bring out his or her personal best by applying methods developed by behavioral science. Wellness coaching assists clients in:

- Staying focused on personal needs, values, and vision.

- Defining personal health care habits and wellness practices.

- Developing an action plan to sustain wellness.

- Exploring meaning and, if desired, spiritual wellness.

- Working through the inevitable changes and obstacles that might arise in life.

- Maintaining a healthy balance between one's personal and professional life.

- Bringing out one's best to achieve personal peace.

Unlike psychoanalytical therapy, which addresses past issues and situations, wellness coaching focuses on the present. Such coaching also looks toward the future and what clients want to accomplish in order to reduce stress, sustain a healthy lifestyle, and achieve success.

Who becomes a wellness coach? The answer is fitness professionals, doctors, social workers, meditation instructors, spiritual consultants, career specialists, massage therapists, psychologists, counselors, and many other professionals whose job it is to help their clients achieve good health and success in life.

WORK ENVIRONMENT

Wellness coaches work with individuals in their homes, in offices, by telephone, or even by e-mail. Wellness coaches also work in the corporate environment. Here, they help employees get the most out of their lives while at the same time maximizing creativity and productivity. Some wellness coaches write books and articles in addition to working with clients. Some teach seminars and classes and work with doctors, dieticians, and other health professionals.

Of course, wellness coaches who are also personal trainers or group fitness instructors will share the same kinds of working environments as others in those careers: personal gyms, the homes of clients, fitness centers, corporate fitness centers for employees, and medical settings.

CERTIFICATION

There are many coaching certifications and degrees available. In the back of this book is a list of certifying agencies and contact information. Below are a couple of examples including the educational curriculum.

Wellcoaches Corporation (http://www.wellcoach. com) trains health and fitness professionals, offers wellness coaching to employees of corporations, and provides fitness centers and hospital wellness centers with services that will help members improve their wellness. Wellcoaches contends that its coaching methodology and content are based on the best practices available today. Its approach to wellness includes stress management, nutrition, physical activity, and weight management, as well as health and life issues that impact wellness. Wellcoaches' program is designed specifically for the Internet. Wellcoaches' ten-week training program includes the following lesson content:

- Introduction to wellness coaching
- Client relationship skills
- Behavior change
- Navigating the Web coaching platform
- Client assessment
- Conducting coaching sessions
- Setting goals
- Overcoming obstacles
- Practice client review
- Marketing

The Wellcoaches program is accepted as thirty continuing education hours toward an American College of Sports Medicine (ACSM) recertification, and 1.9 American Council on Exercise (ACE) continuing education credits.

The Spencer Institute is an organization that provides business development, training, certification, and support for individuals who want to help others achieve peak performance in life. The Spencer Institute program teaches students how to coach and mentor individuals, couples, groups, and organizations on a variety of life strategy topics. Upon completion of the training program, you will hold the title of Certified Life Strategies Coach. The Life Strategies Coach curriculum includes:

- **Stress management:** How to create a relaxing environment for you and your client. You will learn simple and effective breathing techniques and restful postures.

- **Your image:** Learn about proper dress, hairstyle, and business etiquette.

- **Organizational skills:** Discover how to get organized and help others to do the same.

- **Smart nutrition:** Develop the base knowledge to offer sound nutritional facts to your coaching clients.

- **The Spencer method of wellness:** Learn the principles of mind-body fitness and wellness.

- **Developing your coaching Web site:** Learn how to make the most of your Web site to begin a worldwide coaching practice.

- **Domestic violence awareness and prevention:** Learn the signs and triggers of domestic violence.

The Spencer Institute program is approved by the American Council on Exercise for fifty continuing education credits and by the International Sports Science Association (ISSA) for twenty continuing education credits.

SALARY RANGE

According to the Spencer Institute, the average coach makes roughly $350 a month per client in the United States.

Summary

Job Description
Wellness coaches guide and motivate clients to reach their peak fitness potential by developing customized fitness plans based on an assessment of the client's fitness needs and wants. While most fitness career certifications focus on exercise, wellness coaching goes beyond this to deal with the whole client—including not only the body, but the mind.

Necessary Education
Wellness coaches must have two years of experience practicing as a health or fitness professional, and working with clients or patients (either part-time or full-time). Also, to be qualified for a wellness certification program, coaches should at least have either an associate's degree or a bachelor's degree in exercise, nutrition, or a related field.

Helpful High School Courses
Physical education, health, biology, English, mathematics, and business courses.

This is for four forty-five-minute coaching sessions per month. If you are doing corporate coaching, you can expect to earn between $150 to $200 per hour. It is not uncommon for a seasoned coach to earn well over $100,000 per year. Most coaches ask for a minimum of a three-month commitment to their coaching program.

CAREER PATH

You should begin by studying physical education, health, biology, English, mathematics, and business courses while you're in high school. This will give you a solid foundation from which to start.

Though at the time of publication there were no educational prerequisites to becoming a wellness coach, Wellcoaches requires two years spent practicing as a health or fitness professional, aside from working with clients or patients (either part-time or full-time). Also, at least either an associate's degree or a bachelor's degree in exercise, nutrition, or a related field is necessary. An acceptable alternative would be certification from a nationally recognized certification program, such as the American College of

Sports Medicine, the American Council on Exercise, the National Strength and Conditioning Association, or the Aerobics and Fitness Association of America.

If you want to work for yourself, start thinking about a plan for marketing and attracting clients. You may want to associate yourself with a few fitness centers that could benefit from having a wellness coach available. It's a good idea to build a network of friends, associates, and others— even with medical professionals—who might offer a referral system for building a client base.

If you plan to work as an employee at a health club or in a medical setting, you'll want to think about preparing a good résumé. You'll also want to make sure that you're a good example of someone who has personally benefited from the practices a wellness coach can offer.

CHAPTER 7

EXERCISE SPECIALIST

A ccording to the Centers for Disease Control and Prevention (CDC), during the past twenty years there has been a dramatic increase in obesity in the United States. In 1991, four states were reporting obesity rates of 15 to 19 percent and no states reported rates at or above 20 percent. In 2002, twenty states had obesity prevalence rates of 15 to 19 percent; twenty-nine states had rates of 20 to 24 percent; and one state reported a rate of more than 25 percent.

At the same time, missing from the schedule of many students is one class that used to be a given: physical education (PE). From North Carolina to Hawaii, gym classes have been squeezed out of the school day. This is a trend that parallels a national increase in childhood obesity. In 1991, four in ten high-school students took daily PE classes; ten years later, the proportion was reduced to barely one-third. In 1980, just 5 percent of school-age children were severely overweight; twenty years later, the number had jumped to 15 percent.

Most obese people can enhance their quality of life with a well-designed program of physical activity. This requires the help of someone with in-depth knowledge of the appropriate type of activity that will be the most beneficial. That person is an exercise specialist.

In light of the statistics mentioned above, we should not be surprised to learn that millions of Americans suffer from chronic diseases related to poor physical fitness, such as:

- Heart disease
- Hypertension
- Arthritis
- Osteoporosis
- Anxiety and depression
- Back pain
- Diabetes
- Obesity

In addition to working with special populations who are able (or who can learn how) to be physically active, an exercise specialist can also form an important bridge between rehabilitation clinics and a health club or home-based exercise program. In conjunction with other health care professionals, exercise specialists know how to design, implement, and manage exercise activities and appropriate lifestyle programs for individuals undergoing rehabilitation for chronic disease. These include those mentioned above, as well as musculoskeletal (referring to the muscles that produce bodily movements) injury and/or disability.

There are several different kinds of exercise specialist certifications both in the United States and Canada. This includes post-rehabilitation exercise specialists and clinical exercise specialists. There are also certifications for personal trainers who work with seniors. Regardless of the type of certification, the best exercise specialist programs all have a common knowledge base and educational prerequisites. The extensiveness of information available is beyond the

Professional Behavior

Below is breakdown of what will be expected of you in your work environment.

1. A professional shows up on time and is prepared. Nothing is more unprofessional than to arrive late. Be dependable. There are no second chances.

2. Have some pride in how you present yourself. Be well-rested. Dress appropriately. If you will be demonstrating workout techniques, wear loose, comfortable, clean attire that is not threadbare or full of holes. If you expect to be treated as a professional, present yourself professionally.

3. You should be courteous and open to any questions your client may have. Your client should feel like you're an ally in his or her efforts to solve a problem.

4. Be willing to listen and learn. Having an arrogant, know-it-all attitude will be your downfall. There is always something new to learn and an old habit to break. Continue your fitness education. Stay abreast of current trends, research, and methods of training by attending workshops, reading industry publications, and taking classes. A professional grows with the changing times.

continued on page 81

limitations of this chapter. The information that follows will give you a good general idea of what exercise specialists do, what is necessary to be prepared for an exercise specialist certification program, and what kinds of things you'll be expected to learn along the way.

WORK ENVIRONMENT

Exercise specialists may find themselves working in many different environments. Possibilities are the specialist's own professional home gym, a client's home, a fitness center, or a rehabilitation facility. You will be regarded as a professional and should expect to dress and behave like one. You can expect to spend hands-on time with clients and also to devote time to meticulous record keeping and other administrative work.

CERTIFICATION

There are many different kinds of exercise specialist certifications in the

United States and Canada. In Canada, a certified exercise therapist is similar in many respects to an exercise specialist in the United States. Canadians may want to start with the Canadian Society for Exercise Physiology (CSEP), which is a not-for-profit organization. You will find contact information for CSEP, as well as many other Canadian and U.S. fitness organizations, in the back of this book.

The following prerequisites and educational content of two U.S. certifying agencies will give you a general idea of what you can expect to encounter in most of the certification programs in the United States and Canada.

5. If you're working within or alongside a medical facility, be aware of rules and regulations for exercise specialists. Follow them. It is your duty to be a team player and abide by these policies.

6. Your client is purchasing expertise and treatment. You owe your client quality care in return. As in medicine, there is no guarantee of a "cure." However, as in medical care, the first rule is "do no harm."

7. You cannot release any information about your client without his or her express written consent.

8. A therapeutic relationship can be an intense relationship, but it is never a social relationship or a sexual one. Sexual overtures from a therapist are not ethical under any circumstances.

American Fitness Professionals and Associates (AFPA) offers a post-rehabilitative exercise specialist certification. According to its Web site (http://www.afpafitness. com), in this program you will learn "how to develop safe and effective post rehab fitness programs for clients with various limitations that are recovering from a variety of injuries, disease and/or treatments." The AFPA's post-rehabilitative exercise specialist certification program covers the following topics:

- Background and definition of post-rehabilitation and various injuries

- Managed care and post-rehabilitation conditioning
- Liability concerns in rehabilitation conditioning
- Post-rehabilitation conditioning of the shoulder
- Post-rehabilitation conditioning of the lower back
- Post-rehabilitation conditioning of the knee
- Post-rehabilitation conditioning of the lower legs, feet, and ankles
- Post-rehabilitation conditioning for special populations

Here are the minimum suggested prerequisites for the AFPA's post-rehabilitative exercise specialist certification program:

- You should be eighteen years of age and have a high school diploma or equivalent.
- You should have 400 documented hours (on letterhead) of hands-on training from a supervisor.
- You should hold a personal trainers certificate or equivalent from a nationally recognized organization.
- You should have a basic understanding of anatomy and resistance/cardiovascular training.
- You should have a basic familiarity with resistance-training equipment.
- CPR certification may not be required to take the examination but it may be required by an employer or in order to obtain liability insurance.

The American Council on Exercise (ACE) offers a clinical exercise specialist certification program. Clinical exercise specialists train in the following areas:

- **Screening and assessment:** You will learn how to establish a rapport with your client. You'll learn how to use questionnaires and conduct interviews. You'll also gain experience in consulting with physicians and other health care providers in order to gain the information you'll need to design an appropriate program of physical activity for each client. You'll also learn how to identify each client's readiness, expectations, and personal preferences. This will aid you in program design. You'll study how to perform baseline and follow-up evaluations of physical activity levels and physical limitations. To do so, you will use recommended guidelines and established protocols to ensure safety and monitor effectiveness.

- **Program design:** You will study how to establish realistic and measurable short- and long-term goals. You'll do this by acknowledging the client's expectations and interpreting assessments and reassessment data to design and/or modify a safe and effective program for individuals with existing special health needs. You'll find out how to interpret ongoing assessment data in order to develop safe and effective programs for individuals with chronic disease and/or disabilities.

- **Program implementation and management:** You will discover how to direct your client to a customized program. This will set the foundation for program implementation. You will learn motivational skills and strategies that will enhance compliance with the programs you design. This will maximize the effectiveness of the program. Expect to encounter training in the use of health, clinical, and performance measures. These will aid in program modification and ensure safety and effectiveness. Also covered will be how to attend to your client's changing needs. You will have to learn how to be aware of when to consult with a client or when to refer your client to other health care providers. This is why you'll also need to learn how to properly document your client's program activity and health status. By means of accurate and up-to-date documentation, you will be able to communicate with other members of the treatment team.

The following eligibility requirements are for the American Council on Exercise Clinical Exercise Specialist certification exam:

- You must be at least eighteen years old.

- You must hold an adult CPR certification and it must be current at the time of the exam.

- In order to take the Clinical Exercise Specialist Certification exam, you must have 300 hours of work experience designing and implementing exercise programs for apparently healthy individuals and/or high-risk individuals. This will have to be documented by a qualified professional.

- You must also have a four-year (bachelor's) degree in an exercise science or related field, a current ACE Personal Trainer certification, or another ACE-approved certification (ACSM, NSCA, NASM).

SALARY RANGE

According to the American Council on Exercise 2003 Salary Survey, full-time (forty hours per week) clinical exercise specialists made between $30,000 and $35,000 per year. As employees, they reported benefits such as a health plan, dental coverage, life insurance, a 401(k) program, paid vacations, and sick pay.

CAREER PATH

Begin by studying physical education, health, biology, English, mathematics, and business courses while you're in high school. You must hold a current adult CPR certification before you can take most certification courses. Hence, it's best to get this certificate while you're in high school. A first aid certification may be required or is strongly suggested. This is another certificate you can get while in high school.

Since you must have experience designing and implementing exercise programs, you may want to think about obtaining a group fitness instructor certification and then getting some hands-on experience working in the field. If you enjoy the sciences as well as fitness and think that you may be interested in biomechanics, the next step would be a college diploma. This will increase your employability and chances of obtaining a higher-paying job.

After you have some experience as a certified group fitness instructor (or personal trainer), think about advancing your career by getting an exercise specialist certification. Once again, think about the choices you have for certification agencies. Check the list in the back of this book. Make some telephone calls. Ask some questions. Remember that if you are certified by a highly regarded organization with strict educational guidelines and a comprehensive educational program, you will be acknowledged by your professional peers as having the credentials to work with special populations.

Once you have your exercise specialist certification, you'll need to decide if you want to work for yourself, or for someone else. If you want to work for yourself, one of the most important things you can do to help your career along is to network. Every time you meet someone new, be aware that this person could need your services, know someone who could use your services, or know a doctor who is looking for a well-trained and certified exercise specialist to work with his or her patients. Introduce yourself to rehabilitation clinics in your area.

It would also be a good idea to learn how to create a business plan for yourself. By going through the process of developing a business plan, you will be forced to focus on the realities of self-employment. You will have to look at nuts-and-bolts details so that you can answer some basic questions. For instance, how many clients must you see per week—at a specific fee, minus weekly expenses—to enjoy the kind of lifestyle you would like to have?

Summary

Job Description
Exercise specialists guide and motivate clients in special populations (such as people with chronic diseases or those in rehabilitation for injuries) in order to reach their peak fitness potential by developing customized fitness plans based on an assessment of the client's fitness, medical, and rehabilitation needs.

Necessary Education
In order to become a certified exercise specialist, you must first have work experience designing and implementing exercise programs. You must also have a four-year degree in an exercise science or related field, or a current approved fitness worker certification.

Helpful High School Courses
Physical education, health, biology, English, mathematics, and business courses.

If you plan to work as an employee at a rehabilitation center, you'll want to think about preparing a professional résumé. You'll be meeting with health care professionals who will want to know only that you're a qualified exercise specialist. Most certifying organizations offer advice on how to prepare for a successful interview. Take advantage of whatever accurate and useful information you can find in order to make yourself stand out from the rest of the crowd.

Make learning a part of your lifestyle, develop a professional attitude, and be compassionate. Regardless of whether you're working for yourself or for someone else, if you focus on these three things—knowledge, professional attitude, and compassion—you'll do well.

When you get your exercise specialist certification, you will be able to make a real difference in the lives of your clients. You will be able to take a leadership role in helping them improve their fitness levels and their quality of life. There is great potential for growth and professional recognition.

CHAPTER 8

FITNESS DIRECTOR

A fitness director is a manager. People who become fitness directors must be very skilled in developing fitness programs, managing staff, and dealing with all financial matters. In addition, directors need to have a strong understanding of exercise principles and practices. Fitness directors are responsible for the development and operation of all physical education and fitness programs wherever they work.

Fitness directors must have the knowledge and communications skills necessary to work with other health and fitness professionals, for example, those who assess and prescribe preventive health programs for diet and exercise, exercise leaders, and support staff. Fitness directors must also interact effectively with clients, vendors, and members of the public. They may work in a variety of settings, including health spas and gyms, weight training and conditioning centers, hospitals, nursing homes, recovery facilities, and corporate employee wellness and fitness centers.

WORK ENVIRONMENT

Fitness directors spend most their time indoors in fitness centers and gyms. Their days are filled with any or all of the following responsibilities: dealing with paperwork, spreadsheets, computers, phone calls, and meetings with employees and the public. A fitness director's management responsibilities may include:

- Hiring and training staff
- Purchasing, maintaining, and scheduling equipment for fitness activities
- Developing, monitoring, and controlling physical education and fitness program budgets to ensure a positive financial outcome
- Establishing objectives and policies in cooperation with the professional staff
- Developing and implementing health/fitness programs that will encourage and motivate members and stimulate membership growth
- Developing an annual health promotion plan, including speakers and incentives
- Writing, designing, and editing a newsletter
- Providing information, facility tours, and orientations to potential members

CERTIFICATION

Fitness director certification programs are offered by:

- The National Exercise Prescription Accreditation, which has been active for two years (as of 2004)
- The Canadian Association of Fitness Professionals, which has been active for eight years (as of 2004)
- The American College of Sports Medicine, which has been active for twenty-five years (as of 2004)

- The Cooper Institute for Aerobic Research, which has been active for thirty-one years (as of 2004)

You will find contact information for these organizations in the back of this book.

The Canadian Association of Fitness Professionals (Can-Fit-Pro) offers a Program Director Specialist-Group Fitness Management Course. Its eight-hour management program is hosted annually as a preconference workshop at Can-Fit-Pro's international conference in Toronto. Topics at the workshop have included:

- Measuring the efficiency and profitability of group fitness programs
- Maximizing attendance and reducing costs
- Refining the role of your group fitness manager
- Recruiting, training, and assessing fitness instructors
- Maximizing studio presentation and layout
- Utilizing marketing and promotional campaigns that deliver referrals and membership sales

The American College of Sports Medicine Health/ Fitness Director Certification Program takes a different approach. The ACSM program is the third step in a three-step health and fitness certification process. This occurs after a college education and work experience have been gained. This program is intended primarily for professional administrators of health and fitness programs.

To achieve the ACSM health/fitness director certification, candidates must demonstrate that they have sufficient health and fitness management experience and possess the following minimum requirements:

- A two-year degree, four-year degree, or master's degree in a health-related field from a regionally accredited college or university

- A minimum of two years (full-time) or 4,000 hours of experience as a fitness manager or director
- Current ACSM health/fitness instructor certification
- Current CPR certification

Recommended skills and knowledge for the ACSM health/fitness director certification are:

- Knowledge of practical skills that are necessary for basic business organization and finance
- The ability to organize and administer health and fitness programs for a variety of persons ranging from those with low-to-moderate health risks to those with controlled diseases
- Knowledge of exercise science including kinesiology, functional anatomy, exercise physiology, nutrition, risk factor identification, fitness appraisal, lifestyle modification techniques, exercise prescription, and injury prevention
- Competence in the knowledge, skills, and abilities (KSAs) required of the ACSM health/fitness director, health/fitness instructor, or group exercise leader

The ACSM's health/fitness director certification is based on a self-paced, self-study program using ACSM educational materials that must be purchased. Examinations are taken at ACSM's regional or national meetings or at testing sites for ACSM certification. The written examination contains approximately 115 multiple-choice questions. Areas covered in the exam are:

- Functional anatomy and biomechanics
- Exercise physiology
- Human development and aging
- Pathophysiology and risk factors

- Human behavior and psychology
- Health appraisal and fitness testing
- Emergency procedures and safety
- Exercise programming
- Nutrition and weight management
- Program administration/management

Candidates are given three hours to complete the written exam.

SALARY RANGE

According to the ACE 2003 Salary Survey, fitness directors made between $35,000 and $40,000 per year. Fitness directors reported receiving benefits such as health and dental care, life insurance, paid vacations, and sick pay.

CAREER PATH

Most positions require a college degree in an exercise field and/or fitness certifications, plus three to five years of experience in the field. At least a year of management experience and a current CPR certification is also needed. You'll also have to be proficient with computers and business software such as MS Excel, MS Word, MS PowerPoint or other equivalent programs.

Begin by studying physical education, health, biology, English, mathematics, and business courses while you're in high school. You must hold a current adult CPR certification before you can take most certification courses. Hence, it's probably also best to get this certificate while in high school. A first aid certification may be required or strongly suggested. This is another certificate you can get while still in high school.

Summary

Job Description
Health and fitness directors are administrative leaders who manage health and fitness programs.

Necessary Education
- A college education in a health-related field
- A minimum of two years (full-time) or 4,000 hours of experience as a fitness manager
- A current health and/or fitness instructor certification
- A current CPR certification

Helpful High School Courses
Physical education, health, biology, English, mathematics, and business courses.

After high school, you can go to college and study for a fitness-related degree, or else a business degree with a minor in a fitness-related field. Think about obtaining a group fitness instructor certification and then getting some hands-on experience working in the field.

You should also explore certification options. You'll need to gain credentials at a respected organization. There is a list of certifying agencies in the back of this book. It's a good idea to speak with practicing trainers. They can offer invaluable insight into the day-to-day mechanics of the profession.

Finding an entry-level position in a club or organization with career growth opportunities can be ideal for learning the business and moving into management.

CHAPTER 9

FITNESS CLUB OWNER

To create a business from nothing—and to succeed at it—requires a level of motivation and perseverance that practically borders on obsession. Once you get your fitness club going, you'll be responsible for organizing, managing, and assuming the risks of your enterprise. On average, small business owners can expect to face two major problems and ten minor problems a day. You'll have to develop criteria, choose between alternatives, and do a lot of guessing. However you look at it, there's a lot to do when you own your own fitness club. And to be realistic, you'll need to keep in mind that you'll end up working more hours than any of your employees.

The rare person who has an overwhelming desire to own his or her business is called an entrepreneur. Usually those who can handle the uncertainty and the amount of work needed to create a business from scratch are optimists. To them, the glass is never half empty. Instead it is half full. It takes undying optimism to survive the false starts, near failures, and disappointments that every entrepreneur faces.

Deciding to go into business with the sole goal of making money is a mistake. Making money and accumulating wealth is usually the by-product of successfully accomplishing some other goal. You need an idea and a dream to provide the push for success, to weather the uncertainty, and to provide the will to work longer and harder than anyone else.

The United States government's Small Business Administration (http://www.sba.gov) put together the following chart that will help you decide if creating your own fitness club is right for you.

Are You Ready?

Is entrepreneurship for you?
In business, there are no guarantees. There is simply no way to eliminate all the risks associated with starting a small business—but you can improve your chances of success with good planning, preparation, and insight. Start by evaluating your strengths and weaknesses as a potential owner and manager of a fitness club. Carefully consider each of the following questions.

Are you a self-starter?
It will be entirely up to you to develop projects, organize your time, and follow through on details.

How well do you get along with different personalities?
Business owners need to develop working relationships with a variety of people including customers, vendors, staff, bankers, and professionals such as lawyers, accountants, or consultants. Can you deal with a demanding client, an unreliable vendor, or a cranky receptionist if your business interests demand it?

How good are you at making decisions?
Small business owners are required to make decisions constantly—often quickly, independently, and under pressure.

Do you have the physical and emotional stamina to run a business?
Business ownership can be exciting, but it's also a lot of work. Can you deal with six or seven twelve-hour workdays every week?

How well do you plan and organize?
Research indicates that poor planning is responsible for most failures in starting up a fitness club or other small business. Good organization—of financials, inventory, schedules, and production—can help you avoid many pitfalls.

Is your drive strong enough?
Running a business can wear you down emotionally. Some fitness club owners burn out quickly from having to carry all the responsibility for the success of their enterprise on their own shoulders. Strong motivation will help you survive slowdowns and periods of burnout.

How will the business affect your family?
The first few years of business start-up can be hard on family life. It's important for family members to know what to expect and for you to be able to trust that they will support you during this time. There also may be financial difficulties until your business becomes profitable, which could take months or years. You may have to adjust to a lower standard of living or put family assets at risk in the short-term.

Where will you find the money to start a new business? If you aren't independently wealthy by the time you have enough experience to start your own fitness club, family members, friends, and former associates are all potential sources. This is especially so when capital requirements are smaller. State and local city governments sometimes offer programs to encourage small businesses, especially if they are to be built in areas that are targeted for growth. Banks, savings and loans companies, commercial finance companies, and the U.S. Small Business Administration (SBA) are other common sources of loans.

Since banks are usually reluctant to offer long-term loans to small firms, the SBA offers a guaranteed lending program that "encourages banks and non-bank lenders to make long-term loans to small businesses by reducing their risk and leveraging the funds they have available." The SBA has been an integral part of the success of thousands of start-ups around the country. You can find contact information for the SBA in the back of this book.

WORK ENVIRONMENT

Fitness club owners will spend most of their time dealing with the constant pressures and complications of running a business. They will often see the inside of their offices much more than they see their weight or aerobics rooms.

CERTIFICATION

There is no certification necessary to become a fitness club owner. However, experience as a certified fitness worker—such as a group fitness instructor or personal trainer—will give you the knowledge you need to run a successful business. In addition, you will need a business education.

SALARY RANGE

According to the ACE 2003 Salary Survey, a fitness club owner makes between $45,000 and $50,000 per year. As a fitness club owner, your income will only be limited by your ability to run and expand a successful business. This is especially true if you are able to expand your original club into a franchise of several clubs.

Fitness club owners can give themselves any benefits they can afford. Some benefits include health and dental coverage, life insurance, a 401(k) plan, paid vacations, and sick pay.

CAREER PATH

For those interested in a career as a fitness club owner, it's best to start with classes that will be helpful in high school such as physical education, health, biology, English, mathematics, and business. Getting involved in leadership is a good idea, too. You might think about working on the school newspaper, getting involved in a school sports club, or joining a debate team. It's also a good idea to volunteer in your local community. This will give you a good deal of experience and an opportunity to build a network of friends and associates that will become valuable to you later. These friends and associates may end up playing a pivotal role when you decide to start your own fitness club. You never know. So make lots of friends—and be a good friend.

You're going to need first aid and CPR certification if you decide to become a certified fitness professional—for example, a personal trainer or group fitness director. It's best to get these certifications while you're in high school. Keep in mind that you will need to be at least eighteen years old to obtain your fitness professional certification.

After high school, think about attending a community college, state college, or university in order to study physical education and business. Consider getting a fitness certification as well. There's no reason why you can't follow through with both of these objectives at the same time.

After you get your fitness professional certification, see if you can get a job at a local fitness center. If you work part-time, you can gain some career experience while you finish your college studies. There is nothing better than working at a fitness center in order to learn how these businesses are run.

Once you've gone through the process of getting multiple professional fitness certifications, once you've got your business degree, and once you've spent a few years in the business as a successful professional, it's time to build a foundation for your dream health club. This means doing your homework. Those who are best prepared and have sound insight into the state of the industry are going to succeed. Get advice from the Small Business Administration and create a business plan.

Parts of a Business Plan

A business plan should be detailed, clear, and concise. It should be no longer than twelve pages, and it should include the following information:

- Executive summary: A very short, concise overview for busy executives.
- Mission statement for the club and a plan for enacting it: A detail of how you plan to operate and grow a successful business.
- Market analysis: A study to show that the local fitness market is growing.
- Competitive analysis: This will show who your competitors are in the local fitness market, as well as indicating how you plan to be competitive.
- Facilities and programs to be offered.
- Management: Explains who your management staff will be.
- Exit strategy: When it comes time to sell your club or if you decide to get out of the business, this part of the plan will show how you will sell or close your business in a financially successful way.
- Appendix: This may include information such as who your consultants are, and whether or not your business is a franchise.

Opening a fitness center without first developing a business plan would be like jumping out of an airplane without first making sure that you have a working parachute. Business plans force you to make sure that your ideas are financially viable. In order to write up a successful plan, you must investigate the local market, be aware of the competition, and have a sense of your expenses versus potential income. Even if you are using family money to start your company, putting time into your business plan will help you make sure that you know what you're getting into.

Financing requires a compelling business plan that helps the club owner get equity, fund debt, and create a roadmap for senior management. The business plan is created for bankers, investors, and senior management—each of whom will want different types of information in the plan.

A banker is interested in the concept and the total cost the club owner's ability to pay back the debt. Investors will want to know what the risk is to them. They are concerned about cost overrun and they'll want to know about working capital, tax benefits, and their returns. Senior management wants to see the operational numbers and plans. A business plan needs all of this information (perhaps in chart format) to satisfy each of these audiences.

SCORE

When it comes time to think about business plans, at no charge to you, Counselors to America's Small Business (SCORE) can be of assistance in determining whether or not your ideas are viable. SCORE is a nonprofit association dedicated to entrepreneur education and the formation, growth, and success of small businesses nationwide. Volunteer counselors work with entrepreneurs through every phase of their venture: generating and assessing ideas, preparing a business plan, raising capital, and managing the operations and finances of a growing venture. SCORE was formed in 1964.

SCORE Association
409 3rd Street SW, 6th Floor
Washington, DC 20024
Telephone: 1-800-634-0245
Web site: http://www.score.org

INTERVIEW WITH A FITNESS CLUB OWNER

Anthony Campeau is a personal trainer and the new owner of the Fitness Zone, which is small fitness center located near Yosemite National Park in central California.

The Fitness Zone offers free weights, weight machines, racquetball courts, a group fitness room, and an area for aerobic exercise equipment. Campeau recently spoke about his career in the fitness field.

What initially attracted you to the fitness field?

Initially, my roommate in college was on the verge of becoming a professional bodybuilder. Before that, I had no interest in weightlifting or fitness of that sort except when I played sports and I was required to lift. I liked the way he looked and I liked the fact that you could manipulate your body with the proper nutrition and weightlifting workouts.

How did you get your start in the fitness industry?

I took a job in a very small gym in Reno, Nevada, working the front desk. My roommate was a personal trainer and I decided that was what I wanted to do . . . So I went out and got my personal training certification and the rest, as they say, is history.

Did you study fitness in college? If so, which school did you go to and which degree did you pursue?

I studied nutrition and exercise physiology. I attended the University of Nevada in Reno. Great school.

When you were studying for a career in fitness, did you ever imagine that you'd have your own fitness center?

It was always my dream to own my own fitness center but I honestly never thought I would. After college in Reno, I started my own personal training business, which did quite well. I was training casino execs' [executives'] wives and people of that sort. [The personal training] business is all word of mouth and if you can find one person who sees results, that person will tell everybody.

What extra knowledge (beyond your fitness background) is needed for operating a fitness center?

Business, business, business! You have to have some business sense or it simply won't work. Just being in great shape isn't enough anymore. You really have to give the people what they want or they will leave. It is that simple.

What is the downside to owning and operating a fitness center?

Really, the only downfall to owning this business is the hours I have to work. I didn't think I was going to work as many hours as I am. But [my wife] Emilie is here working right by my side, so it makes things much easier. Also, if there are any complaints, they fall directly at my feet. But it isn't really that bad. The pros definitely outweigh the cons.

What are the joys of owning and operating a fitness center?

Knowing that I am the boss and I can make any decisions I want is really nice. I am also able to help people get into the best shape possible, which for me is the reason I got into the business in the first place. Taking a person who is fat and unhealthy and turning that person into the person they always wanted [to be] is what this business is all about for me.

Summary

Job Description
A fitness club owner handles staffing, maintenance, membership and member activities, marketing, budgets, and other day-to-day activities associated with running a fitness business.

Necessary Education
Experience as a fitness worker working in a fitness club, plus a college-level education in business studies.

Helpful High School Courses
Physical education, health, biology, mathematics, business, and English courses.

CHAPTER 10

MORE FITNESS CAREER OPTIONS

I f you decide to pursue an advanced degree at a university in sports medicine or exercise science, more career opportunities become available.

According to the American College of Sports Medicine (ACSM) Web site (http://www.acsm.org), "Sports Medicine is the field of medicine concerned with injuries sustained in athletic endeavors, including their prevention, diagnosis, and treatment. The purpose of injury prevention and treatment is to maintain optimal health and maximize peak performance."

In the past, sports medicine was the responsibility of the team doctor, who mostly worked with amateur and professional athletes. Today, however, a team is made up of many professionals, such as athletic trainers, biomechanics, exercise physiologists, and nutritionists.

According to the ACSM, "Exercise science is the study of movement and the associated functional responses and adaptations. In this context, an exercise scientist must understand the scientific basis underlying exercise-induced physiological responses."

Exercise science involves a range of disciplines similar to those in sports medicine; however, the field of exercise science is typically much broader than sports medicine. For example, people with an exercise degree (or degrees) may study how disease has an impact on organ systems in research settings, or find ways to improve the biomechanical efficiency of an employee working on an assembly line.

The American College of Sports Medicine is working with the Commission on Accreditation of Allied Health Education Programs (CAAHEP) to define and establish two allied health occupations—one of which, the Health and Fitness Specialist and Clinical Exercise Physiologist, may cause some confusion. The ACSM clinical exercise specialist program will be different from the American Council on Exercise Fitness exercise specialist certification mentioned in chapter 6. Essentially, the ACSM program will require a master's degree. The health and fitness specialist program requires a four-year degree.

The Commission on Accreditation of Allied Health Education Programs is one of the largest accrediting bodies in the United States. The ACSM was recently approved as an associate member of the Commission on Accreditation of Allied Health Education Programs.

The ACSM defines its new exercise physiologist occupation as someone who will:

[D]eliver a variety of exercise assessment, training, rehabilitation, risk factor identification and lifestyle management services to individuals with or at risk for cardiovascular, pulmonary, and metabolic disease(s). These services are typically delivered in cardiovascular/ pulmonary rehabilitation programs, physicians' offices or medical fitness centers. The ACSM Exercise Physiologist is also [able] to provide exercise related

consulting for research, public health, and other clinical and non-clinical services and programs.

The minimum requirements to qualify for the ACSM exercise physiologist program are:

- A four-year degree in an allied health field from a regionally accredited college or university (one is eligible to sit for the exam if the candidate is in the last term of their degree program)
- A minimum of 600 hours of practical experience in a clinical exercise program (e.g. cardiac/pulmonary/ rehabilitation programs, exercise testing, exercise prescription, electrocardiography, patient education and counseling, disease management for cardiac/pulmonary/ metabolic diseases, and emergency management)
- Current certification in basic life support (BLS)

According to the ACSM Web site, "The Clinical Exercise Physiologist works in the application of exercise and physical activity for those clinical and pathological situations where it has been shown to provide therapeutic or functional benefit." Furthermore, "The Clinical Exercise Physiologist performs exercise evaluation, exercise prescription, exercise supervision, exercise education, and exercise outcome evaluation. The practice of the Clinical Exercise Physiologist should be restricted to clients who are referred by and are under the continued care of a licensed physician." Clients may include those with cardiovascular, pulmonary, metabolic, immunological, inflammatory, orthopedic, and neuromuscular diseases and conditions.

The minimum requirements to qualify for the ACSM clinical exercise specialist program are:

- A graduate degree in exercise science, exercise physiology or physiology from a regionally accredited college or university

- A minimum of 1,200 hours of relevant clinical experience (may be completed as part of the graduate degree)
- Cardiovascular: 240 hours required
- Pulmonary: 60 hours required
- Metabolic: 120 hours required
- Orthopedic/musculoskeletal: 120 hours required
- Neuromuscular: 60 hours required
- Immunological/hematological: 60 hours required
- Additional hours from any of the above: 540 hours required
- Experience in providing clinical exercise services for patients with chronic diseases and conditions

The career possibilities that are discussed in the rest of this chapter are available to people with an undergraduate degree or a graduate degree in exercise science, sports medicine, or exercise physiology.

ATHLETIC TRAINER

When working in cooperation with physicians and other health care professionals, a certified athletic trainer is an integral member of an athletic health care team. Athletic trainers work in secondary schools, colleges and universities, sports medicine clinics, professional sports programs, and other athletic health care settings.

Although athletic training was once considered a male-dominated profession, according to the National Athletic Trainers' Association (NATA) more and more women are becoming certified athletic trainers.

Before athletic practices, athletic trainers tape, bandage, wrap, brace, and perform other similar injury prevention measures. During practices, the athletic trainer evaluates injuries and determines whether to refer athletes to a physician or to manage minor injuries. Athletic trainers must take responsibility for continual communication among the injured athlete, family, physician, and coaches regarding when the athlete can return to sport activities. As specialists in the prevention, recognition, and rehabilitation of injuries incurred by athletes, athletic trainers administer immediate emergency care. Under the supervision of the family and physicians, athletic trainers use their medical, exercise, and sports sciences knowledge to develop a treatment program for the athlete's injury. Depending on the regional level of competition and institutional requirements, some high school athletic trainers may also teach.

The National Athletic Trainers' Association Board of Certification, Inc. (NATABOC) certifies athletic trainers. The NATA is a not-for-profit organization dedicated to improving the health and well-being of athletes worldwide. The association is committed to the advancement, encouragement, and improvement of the athletic training profession. The association sets the standards for athletic trainers through its educational programs. The NATA also publishes the *Journal of Athletic Training*, a quarterly scientific journal, and *NATA News*, a monthly news magazine.

Certified athletic trainers have, at minimum, a four-year degree, usually in athletic training, health, physical education, or exercise science. In addition, athletic trainers study human anatomy, human physiology, biomechanics, exercise physiology, athletic training, nutrition, and psychology/counseling. As the athletic training field has increased in scope, so has the demand for qualifications. While a bachelor of science degree in an exercise-related field is the underlying requirement, most employers now prefer someone with a graduate degree.

The current pay scale for strength and conditioning coaches and athletic trainers ranges from starting salaries of $22,000 (at the high school level) up to more than $200,000 in the National Football League or the National Basketball Association.

BIOMECHANIST

Biomechanics is the study of the laws of physics as applied to physical activity, exercise, and sport. Biomechanics can be used to explain how muscles, bones, and joints are injured under certain conditions and how to improve performance using motion analysis techniques. Biomechanists are typically employed in research settings and clinical sites such as rehabilitation centers.

The minimal requirement to become employed as a biomechanist is a master's degree. Be aware that most work for biomechanists is in academia, where a doctoral degree is required.

There may be some career growth potential for the biomechanist in ergonomics. In this field, a biomechanist would use his or her skills for any or all of the following: preemployment physical capacity screening, job station redesigning to fit the worker (similar to altering sports equipment to fit the athlete), worker training (fitting the worker for the job; technique and movement training, or physical capacity training). Other employers of biomechanists are manufacturers of sports and lab equipment, federal labs (army, navy, air force), and the automotive and aerospace industries.

CARDIOPULMONARY REHABILITATION SPECIALIST

This exercise specialist provides both immediate and long-term guidance for the physical rehabilitation of individuals who, for example, have had a heart attack or heart surgery, or who have emphysema. A major component of this physical rehabilitation is exercise testing and training.

Hospitals hire exercise specialists and require at least an undergraduate degree. However, your chances of employment improve with an advanced degree and/or some type of recognized certification, such as that offered by the American College of Sports Medicine.

KINESIOLOGIST

Kinesiology is a multidisciplinary science encompassing three primary areas of study: biomechanics, exercise physiology, and psychomotor behavior. Biomechanics examines how forces act upon and within your body (or any other biological structure), and the effects produced by these forces. Though in academia there seems to be some controversy about the definition of "exercise physiology," by definition, exercise physiology is the study of how the body's systems react to exercise, stress, activity, and lifestyle. "Psychomotor" pertains to voluntary physical movement, such as walking or jumping. Psychomotor development focuses on the progressive acquisition of skills involving both mental and motor activities, for example, learning how to play racquetball. Physical coordination, balance, reaction time and hand-eye coordination combine to define psychomotor behavior. Kinesiologists use these three primary sciences to study human movement.

Kinesiologists are employed in many different fields. Some help people overcome injuries or illnesses. Meanwhile, kinesiologists working in the rehabilitative field are concerned with maximizing motor and perceptual abilities (such as hand-eye coordination), as well as the individual's total well-being. Kinesiologists are involved in three different rehabilitative fields:

- **Cardiac rehabilitation:** Kinesiologists work with individuals with cardiac problems, such as someone recovering from a recent heart attack. First, a kinesiologist would make a complete assessment of the cardiorespiratory system. This is composed of the heart, lungs, and arteries. The assessment is based on various tests, some of which may stress the heart and lungs in order to see how efficiently they work. Running or walking on a treadmill while being carefully monitored is an example of a stress test. Following the assessment, the kinesiologist would develop a rehabilitation plan that would involve modifying lifestyle behaviors. Suggestions may include a program of exercise, the implementation of a special diet, and suggestions about how to effectively cope with everyday stress. A lack of exercise, a poor diet, and stress are factors in the development of heart disease.

• **Physical rehabilitation:** Kinesiologists use various assessment techniques to allow detailed diagnoses of movement problems. For instance, the kinesiologist will check the range of motion of an arm or leg in order to find out how well a recovering joint, such as a knee or a shoulder, works. If it is discovered that the range of motion is much less than what would be expected for a healthy joint, or if it is found that the joint isn't securely held in place because of loose tendons or weak muscles, a kinesiologist will recommend a program of therapeutic movements. This program must be specifically tailored to the patient's medical problem. Such a program may include stretching and/or strengthening exercises for the muscles, tendons, and ligaments that hold the joint together and make it work properly. The goal is to help the patient regain a full range of motion while at the same time strengthening the joint to help prevent further injury.

• **Special populations in clinical settings:** Kinesiologists working with special populations assess patients and set up rehabilitative programs. The different populations that they may work with may include the developmentally delayed, physically disabled, brain damaged, elderly, or emotionally disturbed. Psychomotor kinesiologists work with patients with autism, cerebral palsy, or other types of perception, neurological, and motor difficulties. They help their patients develop strategies to deal with and improve a lack of motor learning skills that compromises their ability to function.

Some other fields that kinesiologists are employed in are occupational kinesiology and ergonomic kinesiology. In the workplace, there are many complex interactions between the worker, machines, and environment. The study of these interactions is called ergonomics. The basic human sciences involved in ergonomics are anatomy, physiology, and psychology. These sciences are applied toward two main objectives: the most productive use of human capabilities, and the maintenance of human health and well-being. In other words, the job must "fit the person" in all respects, and the work situation should not compromise human capabilities.

For instance, a pianist learns early on to sit up straight and to sit at a proper distance from the keyboard in order to allow his or her arms to be in a comfortable position (with elbows bent and wrists straight). Any other seating position quickly causes fatigue. In an office setting, back pain, shoulder pain, and wrist pain can result from improper adjustment of one's seating position in conjunction with one's keyboard position, monitor position and location of the computer mouse. In a factory setting, joint and muscle pain can be the result of a nonoptimal placement of machines that a worker must use. Repetitive and awkward movements stress joints, muscles, and ligaments because they are forced to move in a way for which they were not designed.

Occupational kinesiologists are concerned with an assessment of these kinds of problems and the recommendation of solutions. Sometimes a new seating position, a lowered keyboard level, a rearrangement of the placement of machines, a change in the quality of lighting, or a redesign of a machine's levers and buttons can greatly increase the well-being of the worker. In turn, this can yield greater productivity and reduce the need for missed work days. Overall, occupational kinesiologists deal with human versus machine interactions, matching skill level with job demands, employee physical fitness, fatigue, health, and safety.

Ergonomic kinesiologists are mostly concerned with assessing the suitability of the design of workstations. They provide suggestions for modifications and assistive devices. For instance, extra tall people sometimes need special office chairs that have an extended seat. This is needed to support longer upper legs. On the other hand, some shorter people need to rest their feet on a foot support under their desk because even the lowest office chairs are too high off the ground for them. Sitting for hours in the wrong office chair without these kinds of assistive devices can cause aches and pains that can have a negative effect on the quality of one's work.

PHYSICAL/OCCUPATIONAL THERAPIST

A physical therapist—usually working closely with a doctor—helps people recover from injuries or diseases of the muscles, joints, nerves, or bone. An occupational therapist works more with fine motor skills and dexterity. Both therapists use various physical modalities and exercise that focus on movement dysfunction. There are many areas of specialization in physical therapy, including:

- Cardiopulmonary rehabilitation
- Sports medicine
- Biomechanics

Most physical and occupational therapy schools require two to three years of education in conjunction with a four-year undergraduate degree. One must also pass a national exam to become a licensed physical or occupational therapist. Most employment opportunities are in hospitals and clinics. Physical/occupational therapists have to know how to do the following:

- Perform tests and evaluations of joint mobility, muscle strength, sensation, functional ability, endurance, and cardiovascular functioning
- Set short- and long-term goals for their patients
- Design individualized treatment plans which may involve therapeutic exercises, endurance training, gait training, training in activities of daily living, massage/soft tissue manipulation, applications of heat and cold, hydrotherapy/wound care, electrical stimulation, traction, and more
- Educate patients and their families in the safe and effective implementation of prescribed treatment plans
- Conduct screenings
- Provide prevention programs to community and work-site groups

The following people can benefit from physical and occupational therapy:

- People who have been injured in accidents (strains, sprains, or fractures)
- People who have experienced strokes, head injuries, or spinal injuries
- People with wounds or burns
- People who have had amputations
- People with multiple sclerosis, arthritis, and other diseases or disorders
- Children with developmental delays, cerebral palsy, spina bifida, or other congenital disorders

- People with work-related injuries
- Athletes who want to prevent sports injuries or those who have experienced such injuries
- People with neck or back pain or other musculoskeletal injuries or conditions
- Postsurgical patients

If you are thinking about a career in physical therapy, you'll have to be a patient person with a genuine interest in people. You'll need to be physically fit and in good health. You'll need to have problem-solving skills and have good communication skills. If you find that you have these qualities, you may be the right person to become a physical therapist.

GLOSSARY

accreditation The granting of approved status to an academic institution by an accredited body after an examination of its courses and standards.

adherence The degree to which an individual follows a given prescribed program; for example, the amount of activity engaged in during a specified time period compared to the amount of activity recommended for that time period.

aerobic With, or in the presence of, oxygen. Aerobic activities are very efficient at producing the basic energy source, adenosine triphosphate (ATP). Aerobic activity can be walking, jogging, biking, exercising, or any activity during which a client is able to maintain a heart rate in the target heart rate zone for a minimum of twenty minutes. Tennis and basketball are not considered aerobic activities.

aerobic exercise Sustained exercise that uses large muscle groups and places demands on the cardiovascular system.

aerobic exercise (training) Exercise with the purpose of developing aerobic or cardiovascular conditioning; activities in which oxygen from the blood is required to fuel the energy-producing mechanisms of muscle fibers. Examples include running, cycling, rowing, and cross-country skiing.

anaerobic Outside the presence of oxygen; not requiring oxygen. Anaerobic activities produce higher levels of lactic acids and carbon dioxide than aerobic activities do. Short duration activities, which require bursts of energy, are usually anaerobic.

anaerobic exercise Short-term, highly intense activities in which muscle fibers derive energy for contraction from stored internal energy sources without the use of oxygen from the blood, but from stored energy sources such as ATP, CP, and glycogen. Examples include short-burst, intense activities, such as sprinting or weight lifting.

anatomy The study of the structure of an organism or its elements; human anatomy refers to the study of the human body.

anterior An anatomical term meaning toward the front. Opposite of posterior.

arthritis Inflammation of one or more joints; a potentially painful disorder that limits a comfortable range of motion. The exercise prescription for arthritis should include slow, controlled exercises that work the full range of motion.

asthma An intermittent obstruction of the tubes that carry air to and from the lungs. Asthma is characterized by episodes of difficulty breathing. For some, asthma is only brought on by exercise. Symptoms of exercise-induced asthma are coughing and shortness of breath after only eight to twelve minutes of movement. Asthma sufferers who wish to exercise should consult a doctor and obtain an exercise prescription.

atrophy A decrease in cross-sectional size of a muscle.

autism A severely incapacitating lifelong developmental disability caused by physical disorders of the brain. Autism typically appears during the first three years of life. It occurs in approximately fifteen out of every 10,000 births and is four times more common in boys than girls. Symptoms include disturbances in the rate of appearance of physical, social, and language skills and abnormal responses to sensations. Any one or a combination of senses or responses can be affected: sight, hearing, touch, pain, balance, smell, taste, and the way a child holds his or her body. Speech and language are also absent or delayed. However, specific thinking capabilities might be present. Autistic people have abnormal ways of relating to people, objects, and events.

axis of rotation An imaginary line or point around which an object rotates.

basal metabolic rate (BMR) The number of calories consumed by the body while at rest. BMR is measured by the rate at which heat is given off, and it is expressed in calories per hour per square meter of skin surface.

biochemistry The study of the chemistry within biological organisms.

biomechanics The study of internal and external forces that act on the body and the effects produced by these forces; the study of the mechanical aspects of physical movement—for example, torque, drag, and posture—all of which are used to enhance athletic technique.

body mass index (BMI) A formula that relates a person's weight to his or her height. The formula is: kg/m*m). Kg is the person's weight in kilograms, and m*m is the person's height in meters squared.

burn The sensation in a muscle when it has been worked intensely. The chemical by-products of fatigue and microscopic muscle tears cause burn.

cardiopulmonary Pertaining to the heart and lungs.

cardiorespiratory Referring to the way that the heart, lungs, and blood vessels work together to deliver oxygen to the body and remove unwanted waste products such as carbon dioxide.

cardiorespiratory endurance The ability to perform large muscle movement over a sustained period of time and the capacity of the heart-lung system to deliver oxygen for sustained energy production. Also called cardiovascular endurance.

cardiovascular Referring to the heart (cardio), the blood, and the blood vessels (vascular).

cardiovascular endurance capacity Overall body endurance or stamina.

catabolism Tearing down or the destruction of body tissue.

cerebral palsy A group of medical conditions that affect neuromuscular functioning.

certification The act of attesting that an individual or organization has met a specific set of standards. Fitness certifications are established by organizations within the fitness industry.

circuit training A method of weight training that incorporates from ten to twelve exercises that benefit the complete body. These exercises are performed in succession with short rest periods. As a result, anaerobic and aerobic benefits are received.

circuit weight training A routine that combines light- to moderate-intensity weight training with aerobic training. A circuit routine typically consists of from ten to fifteen (weight) stations set up at close intervals. The object is to move from station to station with little rest between exercises until the entire circuit has been completed.

compound movements Consists of movement in two or more joints. It is achieved by using two or more muscles to raise a weight.

concentric A muscle action in which the tension developed causes visible shortening of the muscle.

contraction In weight training, the drawing together and thickening of muscle tissue during an exercise.

cut up A term that describes muscles that are highly developed, the bands of which are clearly visible through the skin of a person with a very low ratio of body fat to muscle.

definition Among bodybuilders, a term that describes well-developed muscles that are highly visible due to an extremely low percentage of body fat in comparison to total body mass.

ectomorph A body type that is characterized by a light build and slight muscular development.

endomorph A body type that is characterized by a heavy, rounded build, often with a marked tendency toward obesity or being overweight.

fatigue A state of increased discomfort and decreased efficiency resulting from prolonged or excessive exertion.

flexibility The ability to flex and extend the body's joints through their full range of motion.

franchise A special privilege granted to an individual or a corporate group of individuals by means of a government grant; a franchise to operate one of a chain of fitness clubs.

hypertrophy The increase in size of a muscle as a result of high-intensity weight training.

immunological Referring to the branch of medical science that deals with immunity to disease.

independent contractors Individuals who conduct business independently on a contract basis and are not employees of an organization or business.

inflammatory Characterized by, pertaining to, or causing inflammation.

intensity The amount of force or energy expended during a workout.

interval training A training system in which the intensity levels are changed on a regular basis, allowing a person to gradually attain a higher level of intensity.

isolation movements Movements using one joint and the use of one muscle to raise a weight.

isometric The condition during which movement is produced.

kinesiology The study of human movement.

lean body mass Body weight minus body fat; composed of muscle, bone, and other nonfat tissue.

maximum heart rate The fastest rate at which your heart should beat during exercise. To find your maximum rate, subtract your age from 220.

mesomorph A husky body type with a muscular build.

metabolism The sum total of the energy-production and absorbing processes in the body; the energy used by the body.

motor learning effect An improvement in performance during the initial weeks of strength training due to more efficient motor unit utilization.

motor unit A motor nerve and all the muscle fibers it stimulates; in the quadriceps muscle, one neuron can activate as many as 1,000 fibers. In the eye, where great precision is required, one nerve cell may control only three fibers.

multiple sclerosis (MS) MS is thought to be an autoimmune disease that affects the central nervous system (CNS). The CNS consists of the brain, spinal cord, and optic nerves. Surrounding and protecting the nerve fibers of the CNS is a fatty tissue called myelin, which helps nerve fibers conduct electrical impulses. In MS, myelin is lost in multiple areas, leaving scar tissue called sclerosis. These damaged areas are also known as plaques or lesions. Sometimes, the nerve fiber itself is damaged or broken. Myelin not only protects nerve fibers, but also makes their job possible. When myelin or the nerve fiber is destroyed or damaged, the ability of the nerves to conduct electrical impulses to and from the brain is disrupted. This produces the various symptoms of MS.

neuromuscular Refers to the physiological interplay between the nervous system and the muscles.

obesity A percent of body fat that is greater than 25 percent for males or 30 percent for females.

orthopedics A branch of surgery concerned with the correction of deformities of the skeletal system, especially the spine and its associate structures.

osteoporosis A thinning of the bones. Bone density diminishes as calcium absorption is reduced. Exercised bones become denser and stronger, as long as dietary calcium is adequate.

overload The amount of resistance against which a muscle is required to work that exceeds the weight that it normally handles.

pathological Related to, involving, concerned with, or caused by disease.

periodization Changing training intensity over a period of days, weeks, and months.

physiology The study of essential life processes, functions, and activities.

posterior An anatomical term meaning toward the back. Opposite of anterior.

progression To systematically increase the stress a muscle endures during an exercise. Progression is achieved in one of four ways: by increasing the weight in an exercise, by increasing the number of repetitions performed in one set of exercises, by increasing the number of sets, or by decreasing the rest interval between sets.

pulmonary Of, pertaining to, or affecting the lungs.

repetition or "rep" One repetition of an exercise. Each individual movement of an exercise.

resistance The actual weight against which a muscle is working.

resistance training The use of weights to build lean muscle tissue.

rest interval A pause between sets that allows the body to recover and prepare for the next set of exercises.

routine A defined schedule of exercises, either aerobic or weight training.

set A cluster of repetitions, performed without rest, in a weight-training routine.

spotter Someone who stands nearby to assist another person while he or she is performing an exercise.

static stretching Slowly moving into an extreme range of motion and holding that position for a certain amount of time.

sticking point The point in time when a muscle will resist hypertrophy no matter how hard you work it.

Sticking points are normal. Hypertrophy usually resumes after a short period of dormancy, or if you change your routine.

strength training Exercise specifically designed to work the muscles and make them larger and stronger. See weight training.

stretching Exercise that increases the ease and degree to which a muscle or joint can turn, bend, or reach.

target heart rate In aerobics, the speed at which you want to maintain your heartbeat during exercise.

training to failure Continuing a set until your muscles cannot complete another repetition of an exercise.

warm-up A preworkout routine that prepares the body for more vigorous exercise. It usually consists of light, progressive movements that stimulate the muscles, heart, and lungs.

weight training A form of exercise in which muscles are repeatedly contracted against a weight. Weight training reshapes the body and builds muscle.

workout A planned series of exercises.

FOR MORE INFORMATION

BASIC REFERENCE GUIDES AND HANDBOOKS

CAREER GUIDE TO INDUSTRIES

The *Career Guide to Industries* provides information on available careers by industry, including the nature of the industry, working conditions, employment, occupations in the industry, training and advancement, earnings and benefits, employment outlook, and lists of organizations that can provide additional information. The 2002–2003 edition of the *Career Guide* discusses more than forty-two industries, accounting for more than seven out of every ten wage and salary jobs in 2000. The *Career Guide* is a companion to the *Occupational Outlook Handbook*, which provides information on careers from an occupational perspective.

To order a copy by mail:
Bureau of Labor Statistics
Publications Sales Center
P.O. Box 2145
Chicago, IL 60690

To order a copy online:
http://www.bls.gov/opub/opbform1.htm

To order a copy by telephone:
(312) 353-1880.

To download a copy online:
http://www.bls.gov/oco/cg/home.htm

OCCUPATIONAL OUTLOOK HANDBOOK

The *Occupational Outlook Handbook* is a free nationally recognized source of career information that is revised every two years. It describes what workers do on the job, working conditions, the training and education needed, earnings, and expected job prospects in a wide range of occupations.

To order a copy by mail:
Bureau of Labor Statistics
U.S. Department of Labor
Occupational Outlook Handbook
2002-03 Edition, Bulletin 2540
Superintendent of Documents
U.S. Government Printing Office
Washington, DC 20402

To order a copy online:
http://www.bls.gov/emp/emppub2.htm

To order a copy by telephone:
(312) 353-1880

To download a copy online:
http://www.bls.gov/oco

Those who are interested in being an owner or manager of a fitness club or fitness center may want to contact the following organization:

United States Small Business Administration
Headquarters Office
409 Third Street SW
Washington, DC 20416
(800) U-ASK-SBA (827-5722)
Web site: http://www.sba.gov

CONVENTIONS

The following organizations host international conventions, which offer trade shows, seminars, and networking opportunities for the health club industry.

ECA World Fitness
64 Franklin Boulevard
Long Beach, NY 11561
(516) 432-6877
e-mail: lisa@ecaworldfitness.com
Web site: http://www.ecaworldfitness.com

IDEA, Inc., and IDEAfit.com
6190 Cornerstone Court East, Suite 204
San Diego, CA 92121-3773
(800) 999-4332, ext. 7
Outside the United States and Canada, dial
  (619) 535-8979, ext. 7
e-mail: member@ideafit.com
Web site: http://www.ideafit.com

**International Health, Racquet & Sportsclub
  Association (IHRSA)**
263 Summer Street
Boston, MA 02210
(800) 228-4772 or (617) 951-0055
e-mail: info@ihrsa.org

Sara's City Workout
(800) 545-CITY (2489)
Web site: http://www.saracity.com

CPR AND FIRST AID CERTIFICATION

AMERICAN ORGANIZATIONS

American Heart Association
7272 Greenville Avenue

Dallas, TX 75231
(800) AHA-USA-1 (242-8721)
Web site: http://www.americanheart.org

American Red Cross National Headquarters
2025 E Street NW
Washington, DC 20006
(202) 303-4498
Web site: http://www.redcross.org

CANADIAN ORGANIZATIONS

Canadian Red Cross National Office
170 Metcalfe Street, Suite 300
Ottawa, ON K2P 2P2
(613) 740-1900
e-mail: feedback@redcross.ca
Web site: http://www.redcross.ca

St. John Ambulance National Headquarters
1900 City Park Drive, Suite 400
Ottawa, ON K1A 1A3
(613) 236-7461
Web site: http://www.sja.ca/english

EDUCATIONAL INSTITUTIONS

In the United States, the American College of Sports Medicine (ACSM) University Connection Endorsement Program is designed to recognize academic institutions with educational programs that cover the knowledge, skills, and abilities specified by the ACSM Committee on Certification and Registry Boards. The aim of the ACSM is to prepare students for successful careers in the health, fitness, and clinical exercise programming fields. The following colleges and universities have educational programs approved for endorsement as of spring 2004. The following program curricula cover the knowledge, skills, and abilities expected of an ACSM health/fitness instructor.

Appalachian State University
730 Rivers Street
Boone, NC 28608
(828) 262-2120
e-mail: hiattpm@appstate.edu

Ball State University
710 N. Martin Street
Muncie, IN 47306
(765) 289-1241
Web site: http://prodweb.bsu.edu/prospectivestudents/request.asp

East Stroudsburg University of Pennsylvania
Office of Admissions
200 Prospect Street
East Stroudsburg, PA 18301-2999
(570) 422-3542 or
(877) 230-5547
e-mail: undergrads@po-box.esu.edu

Florida Atlantic University
Office of Admissions
P.O. Box 3091
777 Glades Road
Boca Raton, FL 33431-0991
(800) 299-4FAU (4328)
e-mail: admisweb@fau.edu

Montana Tech of the University of Montana
1300 West Park Street
Butte, MT 59701
(800) 445-TECH (8324)
e-mail: admissions@mtech.edu

Morehead State University
Administration Building
301 Howell-McDowell
Morehead, KY 40351
(800) 585-6781
e-mail: admissions@morehead-st.edu

North Dakota State University
Department of Health, Nutri-tion, and Exercise Sciences
Bentson-Bunker Fieldhouse I
Fargo, ND 58105-5600
(701) 231-8093
e-mail: Pam.Hansen@ndsu.nodak.edu

Northeastern University
Undergraduate Admissions
150 Richards Hall
360 Huntington Avenue
Boston, MA 02115
(617) 373-2200
e-mail: admissions@neu.edu

Ohio State University
Undergraduate Admissions
  and First Year Experience
Enarson Hall
154 West 12th Avenue
Columbus, OH 43210
(614) 292-3980
e-mail: askabuckeye@osu.edu

Santa Fe Community College
6401 Richards Avenue
Santa Fe, NM 87508-4887
(505) 428-1000
**Slippery Rock University
  of Pennsylvania**
1 Morrow Way
Slippery Rock, PA 16057
(800) SRU-9111 (778-9111)
(724) 738-2015
e-mail: james.barrett@sru.edu

**South Dakota
  State University**
Administration 200
P.O. Box 2201
Brookings, SD 57007
(800) 952-3541
e-mail: SDSU_Admissions
  @sdstate.edu

University of Georgia
Undergraduate Admissions
Terrell Hall
Athens, GA 30602-1633
(706) 542-8776
e-mail: undergrad@
  admissions.uga.edu

University of Mary
Office of Admissions
7500 University Drive
Bismarck, ND 58504
(701) 255-7500
e-mail: marauder@umary.edu

**University of Texas
  at Arlington**
701 South Nedderman Drive
Arlington, TX 76019
(817) 272-2011
e-mail: mavmail@uta.edu

**Youngstown
  State University**
One University Plaza
Youngstown, OH 44555
(877) GO-TO-YSU (468-6978)
e-mail: registrar.office@
  cc.ysu.edu

In Canada, there are many universities and college programs in kinesiology and/or physical fitness that can lead to careers in the many professional fitness fields—more than there is room for here. If you are searching for a college or university in Canada, you may want to get some advice from the Canadian Society for Exercise Physiology (CSEP).

EMPLOYMENT AGENCIES AND SEARCH FIRMS

ExerciseCareers.com
(608) 338-5052
e-mail: info@exercisecareers.com
Web site: http://www.exercisecareers.com

FITNESSJOBS.COM
7887 North 16 Street #232
Phoenix, AZ 85020
(800) 259-4397

HealthandWellnessJobs.com
e-mail: scott@HealthandWellnessJobs.com
Web site: http://www.HealthandWellnessJobs.com

H&F Solutions
H&F Solutions specializes in recruitment of management personnel in the fitness industry.
P.O. Box 266
Lincoln, MA 01773
(781) 259-1010

Human Kinetics
P.O. Box 5076
Champaign, IL 61825-5076
(800) 747-4457
e-mail: orders@hkusa.com

Women Sports Jobs
(714) 848-1201
e-mail: Jobs@WomenSportsJobs.com
Web site: http://www.womensportsjobs.com

PROFESSIONAL AND CERTIFICATION ORGANIZATIONS (USA)

Aerobics and Fitness Association of America
15250 Ventura Boulevard, Suite 200
Sherman Oaks, CA 91403-3297
(800) 446-2322
Web site: http://www.afaa.com

American Alliance for Health, Physical Education, Recreation & Dance
1900 Association Drive
Reston, VA 20191-1598
(800) 213-7193

American College of Sports Medicine
P.O. Box 1440
Indianapolis, IN 46206-1440
(317) 637-9200
Regional Chapter: (317) 637-9200, ext. 138
Certification Resource Center: (800) 486-5643
e-mail: certification@acsm.org
Web site: http://www.lww.com

American Council on Exercise
5820 Oberlin Drive, Suite 102
San Diego, CA 92121-3787
(800) 825-3636
Web site: http://www.acefitness.org

American Fitness Professionals & Associates
P.O. Box 214
Ship Bottom, NJ 08008
(609) 978-7583
e-mail: afpa@afpafitness.com
Web site: http://www.afpafitness.com

American Fitness Training of Athletics
P.O. Box 253
Ripley, TN 38063
(866) 312-AFTA (2382)
e-mail: support@aftacertification.com
Web site: http://www.aftacertification.com

Aquatic Alliance International
Web site: http://www.mindspring.com/ ~ aai_getwet

Aquatic Exercise Association
3439 Technology Drive, Suite 6
North Venice, FL 34275-3627
(941) 486-8600 or (888) AEA-WAVE
e-mail: info@aeawave.com
Web site: http://www.aeawave.com

**Aquatic Fitness Professionals
 Association International**
1601 Great Western Drive M3
Longmont, CO 80501
(800) 484-9666, code 5939
e-mail: aquafitpro@aquacert.org

The Board of Certification (BOC)
The BOC is an independent nonprofit corporation that
has been responsible for the certification of athletic
trainers since 1969. The mission of the Board of
Certification is to certify athletic trainers and to identify quality health care professionals for the public
through a system of certification, adjudication, standards of practice, and continuing competency
programs.
4223 South 143rd Circle
Omaha, NE 68137
(402) 559-0091
Web site: http://www.nataboc.org

The Cooper Institute
12330 Preston Road
Dallas, TX 75230
(972) 341-3200
e-mail: courses@cooperinst.org

IDEA, Inc., and IDEAfit.com
6190 Cornerstone Court East, Suite 204
San Diego, CA 92121-3773
(800) 999-4332
Web site: http://www.ideafit.com

International Fitness Professionals Association
14509 University Point Place
Tampa, FL 33613
(813) 979-1925 or (800) 785-1924
e-mail: info@ifpa-fitness.com
Web site: http://www.ifpa-fitness.com

International Sports Sciences Association
400 East Gutierrez Street
Santa Barbara, CA 93101
(800) 892-ISSA (4772) or (805) 884-8111 (international)
Web site: http://www.issaonline.com

National Academy of Sports Medicine
26632 Agoura Road
Calabasas, CA 91302
(818) 878-9203 or (800) 460-NASM (6276)
Web site: http://www.nasm.org

National Association for Fitness Certification
P.O. Box 67
Sierra Vista, AZ 85636
(520) 452-8712 or (800) 324-8315
e-mail: bodybasics@body-basics.com
Web site: http://www.body-basics.com

National Athletic Trainer's Association
2952 Stemmons Freeway
Dallas, TX 75247
(214) 637-6282
e-mail: ebd@nata.org
Web site: http://www.nata.org

National Endurance and Sports
  Trainers Association
29832 Avenida de las Banderas
Rancho Santa Margarita, CA 92688-1835
(877) FIT-NOW-2 (348-6692)
or (949) 589-9166 (international)
Web site: http://www.nestacertified.com

National Federation of Professional Trainers
P.O. Box 4579
Lafayette, IN 47903
(800) SAY-NFPT (729-6378)
  or outside U.S. (765) 471-4514
e-mail: info@nfpt.com
Web site: http://www.nfpt.com

National Fitness Leaders Association
5820 Oberlin Drive, Suite 102
San Diego, CA 92121
(619) 552-2081
e-mail: bhettler@health1.uwsp.edu
Web site: http://wellness.uwsp.edu/nfla

National Strength & Conditioning Association
1885 Bob Johnson Drive
Colorado Springs, CO 80906
(719) 632-6722 or (800) 815-6826
e-mail: nsca@nsca-lift.org
Web site: http://www.nsca-lift.org

National Wellness Association
P.O. Box 827
Stevens Point, WI 54481
(800) 244-8922
Web site: http://www.wellnessnwi.org/nwa

Red Cross Aquatic Instructor Training
(330) 535-2451
e-mail: BaldridgeD@usa.redcross.org

WaterART Fitness Inc. Aqua Fitness Training and Certification
2520 SW 22nd Street, Suite 2–311
Miami, FL 33145
e-mail: info@waterart.org

Wellcoaches Corporation
19 Weston Road
Wellesley, MA 02482
(866) WE COACH (932-6224)
e-mail: info@wellcoaches.com
Web site: http://www.wellcoaches.com

Wellness Coaching Institute
The Wellness Forum
6600 North High Street
Worthington, OH 43085
(614)-841-7700 or (800) 761-8210
e-mail: PamPopper@msn.com

PROFESSIONAL AND CERTIFICATION ORGANIZATIONS (CANADA)

THE CANADIAN SOCIETY FOR EXERCISE PHYSIOLOGY (CSEP)

The Canadian Society for Exercise Physiology (CSEP)
is a volunteer organization composed of professionals

interested and involved in the scientific study of exercise physiology, exercise biochemistry, fitness, and health.

The Health and Fitness Program (HFP) was established by CSEP in 1981 to address certain needs and concerns of personnel working in the physical activity, fitness, and lifestyle appraisal industry specifically "to ensure that quality fitness practices and physical activity counseling services are available to assist in the promotion of an active lifestyle for all Canadians."

HFP certifications include:

- Certified Fitness Consultant (CFC)
- CSEP Personal Fitness Trainer (CSEP-PFT)
- Professional Fitness and Lifestyle Consultant (PFLC)
- CSEP Exercise Therapist(tm)

The HFP has several provincial business offices. Contact the closest office for workshop dates, locations, costs, and renewal/registration information. Residents of Yukon Territory, Nunavut, and the Northwest Territories, contact your nearest HFP business office.

British Columbia
Charleen McBeath
B.C.-FACA
c/o School of Human Kinetics
Room 203B, Osborne Center
University of British Columbia
Vancouver, BC V6T 1Z1
(604) 822-6940 ·
e-mail: contact@csephealthfitnessbc.ca
Web site: http://www.csephealthfitnessbc.ca

Ontario

Patricia Clark/Karen Cooper

Ontario Association of Sport and Exercise Sciences (OASES)

295A Broadway

Orangeville, ON L9W 1L2

(519) 942-2620

e-mail: info@oases.on.ca

Web site: http://www.oases.on.ca

OTHER CANADIAN ORGANIZATIONS

The Canadian Association of Fitness Professionals (Can-Fit-Pro)

P.O. Box 42011

2851 John Street

Markham, ON L3R 5R7

(800) 667-5622, ext. 224

In the Toronto area: (905) 305-8450

e-mail: info@canfitpro.com

Canadian Society for Exercise Physiology (CSEP)

185 Somerset Street West, Suite 202

Ottawa, ON K2P 0J2

(613) 234-3755 or (877) 651-3755

e-mail: info@csep.ca

Web site: http://www.csep.ca

WaterART Fitness Inc., Aqua Fitness Training and Certification

83 Galaxy Boulevard, Unit 19

Toronto, ON M9B 2X6

(416) 621-0821 or (866) 5-GET-WELL

e-mail: info@waterart.com

Web site: http://www.waterart.com

PROFESSIONAL AND TRADE PERIODICALS

ACSM's Health & Fitness Journal
351 West Camden Street
Baltimore, MD 21201
(800) 638-6423
Web site: http://www.wilkins.com

Club Industry Magazine
9800 Metcalf Avenue
Overland Park, KS 66282
(913) 967-1300
Web site: http://clubindustry.com

Fitness Business and Fitness Trainer Canada
Mill Pond Publishing Inc.
30 Mill Pond Drive
Georgetown, ON L7G 4S6
(905) 873-0850
Web site: http://www.fitnet.ca

Fitness Management
3923 West 6th Street #407
Los Angeles, CA 90020
(213) 385-3926
Web site: http://www.fitnessworld.com

Muscle & Fitness Magazine
e-mail: mafcustserv@email.cdsfulfillment.com
Web site: http://www.muscle-fitness.com

FOR FURTHER READING

Bartram, Clark. *You Too Can Be a Fitness Model*. Long Island City, NY: Hatherleigh Press, 2002. A practical guide from one of America's top fitness models.

Brooks, Douglas. *Your Personal Trainer*. Stanninglex Leeds, England: Human Kinetics Europe, Ltd., 1999. Brooks presents the program components and exercise techniques that he prescribes for his clients on a daily basis.

Camenson, Blythe. *Careers for Health Nuts & Others Who Like to Stay Fit*. New York: McGraw-Hill, 2003. All the information you need on salaries, working conditions, and opportunities for professional enhancement.

Fay, Ron. *Small Club Start-Up: A Personal Trainer's Guide*. Candor, NY: Fay's Fitness Company, 2000. *Small Club Start-Up* is a "how-to" book designed to give guidance to personal trainers interested in owning and operating small health clubs.

Gaede, Katrina, Alan Lachica, and Doug Werner. *Fitness Training for Girls: A Teen Girl's Guide to Resistance Training, Cardiovascular Conditioning and Nutrition*. Chula Vista, CA: Tracks Publishing, 2001. Katrina Gaede is a five-time California State Champion gymnast and works as a certified personal trainer. Alan Lachica is a certified USA boxing coach and a certified personal trainer. Doug Werner is the author of all twelve titles in the Start-Up Sports series.

Hammer, Arnold. *Rosen Photo Guide to a Career in Health and Fitness*. New York: Rosen Publishing Group, 1988. Describes ways to make a living in the field of health and fitness.

Huey, Lynda, Robert Forster, and Pete Romano. *The Complete Waterpower Workout Book: Program for Fitness, Injury Prevention, and Healing.* New York: Random House, 1993. An expert presents a detailed water-exercise program for individuals of all fitness levels.

Kaehler, Kathy, and Connie Church. *Teenage Fitness: Get Fit, Look Good, and Feel Great!* New York: HarperResource, 2001. Kaehler is one of Hollywood's most sought-after fitness trainers

Orlick, Terry Ph.D. *Embracing Your Potential.* Champaign, IL: Human Kinetics Publishers; 1998. This book includes insights and quotes from elite athletes, performers, and people in highly demanding jobs. Also features thirty exercises that can help readers make meaningful, lasting changes to boost their performance and enrich their lives.

Plummer, Thomas. *The Business of Fitness: Understanding the Financial Side of Owning a Fitness Business.* Monterey, CA: Healthy Learning, 2003. Thomas Plummer has more than twenty years experience in the fitness industry.

Plummer, Thomas. *Making Money in the Fitness Business.* Los Angeles, CA: Leisure Publications, Coaches Choice Books, 1999. A brutally honest, real-world look at how to become successful in the fitness industry, told by one of the most renowned veterans of the business. Covers conceptualizing the business, the financial foundation, member service, profit centers, staffing, marketing, sales, and more.

Rhodes-Curless, Maura. *Fitness: Careers Without College.* Princeton, NJ: Peterson's, 1992. Find out what it takes to break in to and make your mark as a group exercise instructor, sports massage therapist, sales and service staff member, personal trainer, or floor staffer.

Roberts, Scott O. *The Business of Personal Training.* Champaign, IL: Human Kinetics Publishers, 1996. In

this book you'll find advice on client/trainer relationships, handling clients with special needs, and
marketing and managing your business.

Starkey, Lauren B. *Certified Fitness Trainer Career Starter*.
New York: Learning Express, 2002. A complete "how
to" book for people interested in a fitness career.

Wilson, Robert F. *Careers in Sports, Fitness, and Recreation*. New York: Barron's Educational Series, 2001.
Described here are job opportunities in public and
private health clubs, martial arts academies, public
and private golf courses, sports equipment sales reps
and retailers, and more.

BIBLIOGRAPHY

Aerobics and Fitness Association of America Web site. Various articles. Retrieved 2004 (http://www. afaa.com).

American College of Sports Medicine Web site. Various articles. Retrieved 2004 (http://www.LWW.com/ acsmcrc).

American Council on Exercise Web site. Various articles. Retrieved 2004 (http://www.acefitness.org).

American Fitness Professionals & Associates Web site. Various articles. Retrieved 2004 (http://www. afpafitness.com).

Aquatic Alliance International Web site. Various articles. Retrieved 2004 (http://www.mindspring.com/ ~ aai_getwet).

Aquatic Exercise Association Web site. Various articles. Retrieved 2004 (http://www.aeawave.com).

Board of Certification Web site. Various articles. Retrieved 2004 (http://www.nataboc.org).

Canadian Association of Fitness Professionals (Can-Fit-Pro) Web site. Various articles. Retrieved 2004 (http://www.canfitpro.com/).

Clark, Patricia. Executive Director, OASES and CSEP Ontario Representative. Personal communications. February 9, 2004 through March 22, 2004.

Club Industry Magazine Web site. Various articles. Retrieved 2004 (http://clubindustry.com).

Duke Professional and Personal Development Program, Executive Wellness Coaching Web site. Various articles. Retrieved 2004 (http://www.dukeeap. com/indexb1.html).

IDEA, Inc., and IDEAfit.com Web site. Various articles. Retrieved 2004 (http://www.ideafit.com).

National Academy of Sports Medicine Web site. Various articles. Retrieved 2004 (http://www.nasm.org).

National Athletic Trainer's Association Web Site. Various articles. Retrieved 2004 (http://www.nata.org).

National Strength & Conditioning Association Web site. Various articles. Retrieved 2004 (http://www. nsca-lift.org).

National Wellness Association Web site. Various articles. Retrieved 2004 (http://www.wellnessnwi.org/nwa).

Occupational Outlook Handbook Web site. Various articles. Retrieved 2004 (http://www.bls.gov/oco/ home.htm).

Ontario Kinesiology Association Web site. Various articles. Retrieved 2004 (http://www.oka.on.ca).

SCORE Association Web site. Various articles. Retrieved 2004 (http://www.score.org).

Spencer Institute Web site. Various articles. Retrieved 2004 (http://www.spencerinstitute.com).

Wellcoaches Corporation Web site. Various articles. Retrieved 2004 (http://www.wellcoaches.com).

INDEX

ABOUT THE AUTHOR

Born with asthma and flat, pigeon-toed feet, Randy Littlejohn nevertheless went on to run track in high school, climb to the tops of Mt. Lessen and Mt. Shasta in California and participate in the Great Arcata to Ferndale Kinetic Sculpture Race—twice. Randy continues, at age fifty-five, to work out at least three times a week. His favorite fitness quote, from the Earl of Derby, is, "Those who do not find time for exercise will have to find time for illness."